Catalogs, Services and Portfolios

An ITSM success story

Catalogs, Services and Portfolios

An ITSM success story

DANIEL McLEAN

IT Governance Publishing

Every possible effort has been made to ensure that the information contained in this book is accurate at the time of going to press, and the publisher and the author cannot accept responsibility for any errors or omissions, however caused. Any opinions expressed in this book are those of the author, not the publisher. Websites identified are for reference only, not endorsement, and any website visits are at the reader's own risk. No responsibility for loss or damage occasioned to any person acting, or refraining from action, as a result of the material in this publication can be accepted by the publisher or the author.

Apart from any fair dealing for the purposes of research or private study, or criticism or review, as permitted under the Copyright, Designs and Patents Act 1988, this publication may only be reproduced, stored or transmitted, in any form, or by any means, with the prior permission in writing of the publisher or, in the case of reprographic reproduction, in accordance with the terms of licences issued by the Copyright Licensing Agency. Enquiries concerning reproduction outside those terms should be sent to the publisher at the following address:

IT Governance Publishing
IT Governance Limited
Unit 3, Clive Court
Bartholomew's Walk
Cambridgeshire Business Park
Ely
Cambridgeshire
CB7 4EA
United Kingdom

www.itgovernance.co.uk

© Daniel McLean 2012, 2014

The author has asserted the rights of the author under the Copyright, Designs and Patents Act, 1988, to be identified as the author of this work.

First published in the United Kingdom in 2012 by IT Governance Publishing (978-1-84928-386-1) as *No One of Us is as Strong as All of Us*.

ISBN 978-1-84928-567-4

PREFACE

People often struggle implementing, and operating ITSM processes based on various best practice standards. Rarely is this due to a failure to understand the standards, the tools, or the technology. Usually, it is a failure to appreciate, and deal with, issues surrounding changing people's behaviors.

Implementing process is all about changing behavior. The words in the phrase, *People – Process – Tools*, are in that order for a reason. If People don't embrace the activity, then the Process and Tools won't matter. Changing people's behavior is one of the hardest things we do in business, and something IT people find most difficult.

High-performing IT organizations have a secret to their success. They understand that IT success is more dependent on interpersonal dialogue and behaviors, than on the state of its technology. They have learned how to change behaviors as effectively as they change technology.

Although some best practices mention the importance of being able to change behaviors, they give little specific guidance on how to make it happen.

This is one in a series of books designed to help you do more than just survive these issues. These books will show you how others dealt with the same situations you face every day. Once they learned how to change people's behavior, the process and technology were easy. These books look at what worked, what failed, and traps to avoid.

Learn from their lessons and avoid their mistakes.

ABOUT THE AUTHOR

Mr McLean is a consultant who has designed, implemented and operated processes supporting ITSM for over 10 years. He has worked in IT for over 20 years. He was a peer reviewer during development of the OGC ITIL[1] v3 Service Strategy standard. He has developed and delivered ITIL courseware customized to company-specific operational practices and needs. He has worked in the US and the Middle East.

Mr McLean is the author of *The ITSM Iron Triangle: Incidents, Changes and Problems.*

Mr McLean's consultancy focuses on fusing best practices from multiple ITSM relevant standards, into practical operational processes optimized for each organization's particular environment and needs. He provides this support at the design, implementation and daily operation levels.

Among other honors, Mr McLean holds an ITIL Manager's Certificate in IT Service Management, an ISO20000 Consultant Manager Certificate, and an ISO20000 Professional: Management and Improvement of ITSM Processes Certificate.

Mr McLean holds both Bachelor's and Master's degrees from Cornell University.

Mr McLean resides in Chicago, Illinois, US.

---

[1] ITIL® is a Registered Trade Mark of the Cabinet Office.

ACKNOWLEDGEMENTS

I wish to thank the following people, without whom none of this would have been possible.

My clients, users and customers, for allowing me to learn and improve by serving them.

My managers and leaders, for trusting me with opportunities that made me grow.

My peers, for challenging my habits and making me continually assess and improve my deliverables.

My manuscript reviewers: Chris Evans, ITSM Specialist; ir. H.L. (Maarten) Souw RE, Enterprise Risk and QA Manager, UWV; Charles Araujo, Founder & CEO, The IT Transformation Institute; Susan Schellhase, ITIL Expert, DPSM®, The priSM Institute and President-Elect of the DFW LIG at itSMF US, for their insightful and constructive guidance.

My editors, proofreaders, publishing, marketing and other associates at IT Governance Publishing, for their patience and tireless support; especially Angela Wilde, Publishing Manager.

My teachers and mentors, for their tolerance of my ignorance, persistence in their instruction, and patience with my endless questions. My employees, students and mentees, for allowing me to grow by helping them learn.

My family, for tolerating my single-minded focus.

And my wife, Patricia, for being my rock and constant companion.

CONTENTS

Introduction 1
Chapter 1: Don't Fall Under the Bus 3
Chapter 2: Strange Bedfellows 19
Chapter 3: Don't Confuse me with Facts 29
Chapter 4: Blind me with Science 39
Chapter 5: The Joy of Conflicts....................................49
Chapter 6: Masters of the Universe 59
Chapter 7: How Hard Can it Be?..................................71
Chapter 8: Chow Fun 83
Chapter 9: Help I Need Something 97
Chapter 10: Don't Peek Behind the Curtain...............111
Chapter 11: Know What you Don't Know 123
Chapter 12: A Fool With a Tool is Still a Fool............137
Chapter 13: Boiling the Ocean, a Spoonful at a Time 153
Chapter 14: Change is Hard 163
Chapter 15: No Good Deed Goes Unpunished...........173
ITG Resources 183

Contents

INTRODUCTION

More ITSM initiatives are derailed by the word "service" than any other term you will find. Best practices often talk about service as something that adds value to the business by helping them achieve their goals. In other words, only the business can define what an IT service is. But in most companies, only IT is involved in defining services.

IT tends to look at services from the inside-out, providing offerings to the business in IT terms consistent with the way IT is organized. It maximizes the efficiency of IT and minimizes disruptions in IT.

The business needs services offered outside-in, packaged in terms relevant to their needs and organized in ways consistent with how the business operates.

High-performing IT organizations understand this. Their goal is to be effective in leveraging business operations, as well as efficient in running their operations. To do this, they must offer views of services that are relevant and understandable to their users, as well as useable within IT.

By itself, this is not an overly complex structure. However, establishing this ITSM process, and maintaining it, depends on something that is highly complex – people's behaviors.

Therein lays the challenge for us all.

Please remember that this story has been fictionalized. All persons, places, organizations and events appearing in this work are fictitious. Any resemblance to real people, living or dead, is entirely coincidental. Any resemblance to actual places, organizations or events is entirely coincidental.

CHAPTER 1: DON'T FALL UNDER THE BUS

Ramesh, my boss, seemed strangely nervous as we walked into Lee's office. And that had me worried.

This was the first time I had seen Ramesh anything less than confident in front of other leaders ... at any level.

Lee was a fresh transfer from the field to corporate. That seemed like a bizarre career change, going from sales to IT at a senior management level. You would have thought he'd have figured out what he really wanted to do a long time ago. I didn't know what Lee's real title was yet, only that he was probably close to Ramesh in level.

Ramesh usually treated me like I was one bad decision away from being fired; so it seemed totally out of character that he was dragging me along to what he had confessed was his first meeting with Lee.

But perhaps my recent hard-won success in stabilizing the incident, change and problem processes as the IT service response manager, had changed Ramesh's opinion of me. Maybe this was the first step in his acceptance of me and the value I brought to the team.

Lee said nothing as we walked in, and didn't even rise to offer a handshake. He merely motioned wordlessly to three straight-backed chairs across the desk from him. One of them was already occupied. Lee sat regally on the other side of the desk, a large Cheshire Cat smile on his face.

Ramesh planted himself in the rightmost chair and settled in, before speaking directly to Lee.

"Welcome to IT," said Ramesh. "Tell me about your work in the field."

Lee didn't answer immediately. Instead, he paused and took a long, slow swallow from his coffee mug, then set it down precisely in the center of a marble coaster. A pot of freshly brewed coffee sat on the credenza behind Lee, but he made no effort to offer any to us. With both hands, Lee meticulously slid the cup and coaster to the right side of his large, polished, wooden desk. Printed on the side of the mug were the words, "That Which Does Not Kill Us Makes Us Stronger."

On paper, IT had a business casual dress code, but in practice, it was a lot looser. It probably had something to do with reinforcing what I'd come to believe was the company's cultural view of IT; that we were a group of geeky nerds, with zero social skills and poor personal hygiene, who were kept around because they were the only ones who understood how all those boxes of blinking lights worked. And if you were a high performer, anything that wouldn't get you arrested for indecent exposure, was tolerated and almost expected. It was along the lines of the stranger you looked, the more valuable you must be for leadership to tolerate you. I once saw one of our top security gurus show up to a meeting with no shoes, badly frayed and unevenly cut off homemade, blue jean shorts, and a permanently stained t-shirt that had the words, "Question Authority" drawn across the front with a permanent marker.

Lee was different.

Lee was immaculately dressed in a suit and tie that probably cost more than I made in two weeks. With suit creases sharp as a knife, in a perfect balance of timeless but slightly fashion forward style, he was ready for any occasion. His nails were freshly manicured and clear polished, and every strand of his carefully styled hair was perfectly in place. Lee seemed one of those people who always looked freshly pressed and groomed, even after they'd been flying in a cramped coach airline seat for the last 12 hours. However, I was beginning to suspect that Lee never, ever, flew anything less than first class.

From what I'd heard, he wrapped a positive spin around every comment, and offered a quick response to any question. He had that special chemistry that made you want to like him, and get his approval, even when you disagreed. And if you were to believe the rumors we'd been hearing, he always closed the deal.

Lee occupied a prestigious corner office, with two walls of glass, and an unobstructed view of green lawns and clusters of trees surrounding the property. No parking lot asphalt to interrupt his bucolic vistas. In the distance, the faint outlines of the tallest buildings in the city were visible through the haze. Plaques attesting to great accomplishments cluttered the walls of his office. They formed a tableau, marking his rapid ascension from bag-carrying sales representative to regional director. His rapid advancement, and exposure to many different aspects of the business, hinted that upper leadership was grooming him for a senior role at the company. Maybe that was why he had been pulled out of business operations, brought back to headquarters, and tasked with ensuring IT was doing everything it could to support the success of the field.

I recognized the other person in the seat beside me. His name was Crayton. He was an IT project manager who'd been around for many years. I'd heard he was barely two

1: Don't Fall Under the Bus

years from retirement, and was mostly focused on hanging on long enough to get there. Crayton was the project manager for an initiative called "Sunrise," which was running in parallel to the project I'd been asked to manage, "Rubber Boots." He didn't work for Ramesh. He worked directly for the project management office (PMO). The PMO was where most of our project managers reported. My project was the exception. I couldn't figure out why Lee had invited him to an introductory meeting with Ramesh. It made no sense. Or had Ramesh invited him instead?

I wondered if Crayton had been drafted into owning "Sunrise," like I had been for the "Rubber Boots" project. I still hadn't figured that out. Even though I had no experience, or training, as a project manager, Jason, the senior VP of sales, had insisted I be the project manager for "Rubber Boots," and had done so in front of his peers, and over the objections of our CIO, and my ultimate boss, Jessica. Stranger still at the time, when Jason gave me the task, I'd known him for less than 30 minutes. I must have made a real positive impression for him to trust me with the fate of such an important project as Rubber Boots. Even I had to agree with Ramesh. The risk of me failing with that project was very high.

I'd been around long enough to know that no matter what company you worked at, it was a waste of time trying to understand executive decisions. While sometimes it seemed they made decisions that were good for them and not the company, I had to assume it only looked that way because I didn't have the visibility the executives did. I always assumed good intent on the part of my leaders until proven otherwise. By virtue of their responsibilities, they always place the good of the company above all else. The fact that

I couldn't always see the bigger picture, was why I'd probably never be an executive.

Although I'd never met Crayton before, he was a friend of another project manager I knew from the gym, Maria. She said that despite trying to put himself on "in-house retirement" for the next two years, he'd always been a stand-up guy. From the reports I'd read, his project seemed to be in the same state as mine, on spec, on schedule, and with earned value right on target. But I still didn't understand why he was here … and by himself.

Lee looked up at Ramesh and paused; silently waiting until there were no sounds, except the hum of the air conditioning and Ramesh's nervous breathing.

"Do you know how much revenue I generated in the field last year"? asked Lee.

Ramesh shook his head, "No idea."

Lee wrote a number on a piece of paper, folded it over, and slid it across the desk to Ramesh.

Ramesh looked up at Lee with a slightly shocked look on his face.

"Go ahead," said Lee with a swagger. "You can share it."

Ramesh passed the note to us. I was stunned. It was larger than the entire annual operating budget for IT. So in one sense, Lee had funded IT for the entire company … and more.

"My region was the most productive of any in the company," said Lee. "We supported the largest customer base, had the most renewals, the most new business, the most revenue, and the highest margins. That's why they call us the 'Rainmakers.' We always made the impossible happen."

Ramesh started to speak, "That's very impressive. You must be ... "

Lee cut him off, "So, if my work was so critical to the success of this company, why do you think the executives of this company would take me away from generating the revenue that makes it possible for IT to buy its toys? Why would they bring me back to the home office, thereby putting the company's revenue stream at risk? Do you think the senior executives have lost their minds and want to commit corporate suicide"?

Ramesh just shook his head.

In IT we heard a lot of field people talk about the uselessness of what they saw as a bloated, overstaffed, underused, and generally incompetent, IT organization. They just didn't understand how important we were to their success. They didn't appreciate all the things they didn't see that still had to be done. All they looked at was what they could touch.

It wouldn't have been so bad if they at least showed some gratitude once in a while, but they were always so incredibly ungrateful for all the hard work we did. They never thanked us for all the afterhours work, and all the family time we gave up meeting their crazy deadlines. The only thing they ever did was complain, even if the tiniest thing was not perfect. Maybe the problem was that we were too good at what we did; everything was too seamless. Maybe we needed to fail more often and show them how they couldn't succeed without us. Maybe that would change things.

"Of course you don't know why senior leadership is doing this," said Lee. "That's why you are a mere manager. And why should leadership tell you? After all, you're sitting there and ... ," Lee gestured at his office and the view from his window, "And I am sitting here." Lee rearranged his coffee cup slightly, so that the handle was now precisely parallel to the edge of the pristine blotter on his desk. "Let me tell you why. They did it because they don't want 'good.' In fact, they don't even want 'great.' What the executives of this company want is a game changer, and I am just the leader to make that happen."

Out of the corner of my eye, I caught Crayton staring intently at Lee and rapidly scribbling notes.

Ramesh leaned forward, towards Lee, and said, "That sounds great. There's nothing that can't be improved." Ramesh turned in his chair and gestured at a large collection of awards and trophies. "And I am sure there is a lot you can teach us. I'm sure everyone in IT will support your efforts any way we can."

"I'm glad to hear you say that, Ramesh, because your organization, the whole IT organization, is going to be involved in this."

"Really? Can you share a little of what you need from us, so that your organization and mine can work well together"?

Lee shook his head, smiled, and leaned back in his leather chair. He interlaced his fingers and said, "Sorry, even if you were here by yourself, I couldn't disclose all the details to you yet. Only senior leadership has been briefed on my plan at this point, and they support it enthusiastically. But don't worry. You and your staff will be briefed at the appropriate times, along with the rest of IT. Let's just say that there will be a lot of changes. We're going to infuse IT with the dynamism found in field operations to make it a more productive and responsive organization. No more of this bohemian enclave for losers. We will become the company leaders and a role model for all to follow."

Lee leaned forward and gestured for Ramesh to lean close across the desk. In a quiet voice, Lee asked, "You have heard of the projects named Rubber Boots and Sunrise"?

Ramesh gave an exaggerated look around the room that almost made me laugh. It was as if he were looking to make sure there were no industrial spies hiding in the corners, ready to steal any information they could get.

If Lee caught Ramesh's cartoonish gesture, he didn't reveal it. He simply said, "Although it is premature, I can tell you that the first step will be for me to take personal control of these new projects, and make adjustments to ensure the corporation gets value for its investment, and the field gets maximum utility from the results. And all of it delivered on time, with the content the business needs."

Ramesh interrupted and gestured at me. "But Jason specifically asked for Chris and Crayton to lead these projects. I know. He told me directly."

That answered one of my questions. So Crayton had been drafted, just as I had. Perhaps I now had a compatriot to work with this time. Partners were funny things. Sometimes they could do some of the work, but all too often I found their work not up to my standards, and ended up doing their work, too. Then you were always faced with the moral choice of giving them credit for the accomplishment, because you were supposed to be working as partners, or cutting them off like they deserved.

Lee looked straight at Crayton and myself for a moment, freezing us with his Cheshire Cat smile, before turning back to Ramesh.

"I'm sure these two are both good workers, but obviously neither has experience meeting business critical deliverables under pressure, and definitely are without experience in working with the field or senior leadership. That's why Jason approved this transfer of responsibility. Feel free to confirm it with him at your next scheduled one-on-one with him."

Lee paused for a few seconds, and then added, "Oh, I forgot, you don't meet regularly with him. Well, I do, and you can trust me when I say, he approved it."

Ramesh took a deep breath before saying, "I'm meeting with Jessica later this week. I will wait and confirm with her … "

Lee cut him off. "That will only be a waste of your, and her time. Trust me. This is for Crayton's and Chris' own good. Better to be apprentice to the master longer, than reach beyond one's grasp and fail." Lee stood up and walked to the window, while slowly sipping his coffee. His back to the room, he said, "Learn how to adapt, improvise, overcome. That's what winners do. Just look at me. Model your behavior after me."

Lee turned around quickly, and gesturing to the door said, "Chris … Crayton? Will you please give us some time? Ramesh and I have a few more items to discuss."

Ramesh nodded. As I stood up, Crayton finished writing the last of his notes. Collecting his material, he stood up, and we both headed for the door.

Just as my hand touched the doorknob, Lee added, "Guys … Please don't do anything related to the projects unless I personally review and approve it. Be prepared to give me a full debrief very soon. You will receive further direction on your duties and role here at that time. Thanks."

I was out the door first, with Crayton right behind me. Just before Crayton pulled the door closed, I heard Lee say to Ramesh, "Let me make this very clear. The bus is leaving for success town and you can be on the bus with me, or you can be under the bus with the rest of the losers. The choice is yours. But you have to decide, and decide now. Just understand what it means to be on the bus with the winners. You will need to … "

Crayton pulled the door closed and cut off the last of Lee's words. As Crayton's hand left the handle, he looked at me, shook his head, and said, "I wish I had his energy. What a driver."

I didn't know Crayton well enough to know if he were being sarcastic, or really felt that way, so I simply said. "Let's go to the break room and get a cup of coffee."

Crayton nodded, and added, "I could do better with something stronger."

The break room was empty, and the last person to take a cup of coffee had left the pot nearly dry. The remaining coffee had boiled down into a thick dark sludge that clung to the bottom of the glass pot. Crayton grabbed the carafe and began rinsing it out to make some fresh.

I sat down, and Crayton joined me as the fresh coffee dripped.

"Well that really sucked," I said. "I know everyone was happy with my project, and from what I read, yours, too. Why do you think they asked for a gunslinger to be brought in"?

"I hate to disappoint you," said Crayton. "But you and I, while seeming important in our world, are at the noise level when you talk about executives. It could be any reason. Maybe they are testing Lee, to see if he should be promoted above regional director. Maybe he torqued-off some executive, but since he is a producer, this is their way of punishing him, without losing him. You've gotta think big and broad when that level of leadership is involved. It's a whole different universe. And in the end, you will never know. But above all, you need to work with their direction, not against it. Even in the most extreme scenarios of punishing Lee by the executives, Lee still has the ability to squash us if we get out of line. Remember, he can always be put back in the field and produce revenue. At the end of the day, revenue is the one thing every executive pays attention to. And if he does that, the executives won't really care what he does to us, because we are too far down the food chain for them to recognize we even exist."

"Thank you for restoring my faith in the meritocracy," I said.

Crayton laughed. "I think I'm going to like working with you, Chris, you have a sense of humor."

I smiled, but wished I could see something funny in the situation.

"Besides," said Crayton. "Lee must be doing something right. Did you see all those awards and citations? Maybe we can learn something from him ... something that will help us be left alone for a while. If I were you, I'd try to put a positive spin on things. No sense in missing the opportunity bus when it stops by. In a few months, the projects will be done, and Lee will be off to something else. That's one thing I learned about these types like Lee. They can't stay in one spot very long. Give it a few months, and he'll be off messing in someone else's life."

I was hardly convinced. Crayton could try to sugar-coat it anyway he wanted, but no matter how it was messaged, this change was going to look like I had been demoted because something wasn't right and I couldn't cut it leading the Rubber Boots project. If Crayton was happy with this change, that was his business. He was effectively a short-timer, so his opinion didn't really count.

What made this even more frustrating, was that Lee had smoothly put himself into a position where he could only succeed. I was guaranteed to be the patsy. If Rubber Boots succeeded, Lee would get all the credit, because he dropped in and saved it from my incompetence. If the project failed, Lee would avoid the blame, simply by positioning it that my incompetence had messed it up so bad, no one could save it, not even Lee, the rainmaker.

Lee didn't even need me anymore. He could fire me today and still be able to blame it on me if he wanted. That wasn't fair to me, or anyone else who'd worked so hard on the project, and probably wasn't the right thing for the company either. But it was perfect for Lee, and in his mind that was probably all that mattered.

Crayton poured us both cups of coffee.

I leaned over the table and said, "Look, we've done a great job managing these projects, and if this turkey thinks he is going to step in and take the credit away at the last minute, he needs to rethink it. My manager won't support it. I'm not going to support it. And Lee may find that making things work properly, and getting the right level of co-operation from everyone, just became a whole lot harder than it used to be ... if you know what I mean."

Crayton wobbled his head. "As long as we're still including all the requested functionality and meeting our dates, I'm with you. I just don't want to."

I took a big slurp of coffee. As I set the cup down, a hand came down on my shoulder. I looked, and immediately recognized the well-manicured nails. I turned my head, and standing behind me was Lee, in all his sartorial perfection, that empty Cheshire Cat grin still pasted on his face. It seemed to be his default expression. If Lee had heard our conversation, he gave no indication.

"Hi there. Sorry I had to push you both out of the room earlier, but I needed to have some confidential talks with Ramesh, and I didn't realize you were going to run away." Lee gave a little chuckle, apparently finding something amusing in his comment.

Lee turned to me, and gestured toward the break room door. "Chris, we need to have a serious discussion. I want a briefing on Rubber Boots and I need to discuss some other items with you. Please come back to my office and we will do that now." He picked up my half finished cup of coffee and sniffed at it. Turning up his nose he said, "Why don't you leave that ... beverage ... here. I have some real coffee ... a nice blend of Kona, Indonesian and French Roast, that you might enjoy trying. The beans were freshly roasted this morning."

As Lee led the way out of the break room, I took a quick look back at Crayton, who was smirking. I couldn't tell if that was because he wanted to spend more time with Lee, or felt lucky he didn't get tagged to go first. All I knew is that I felt a little like a condemned prisoner being led to the execution chamber.

I sure hoped I was wrong.

Tips that would have helped Chris

Changes in management will happen for reasons unrelated to your ITSM efforts, yet they will have the potential to impact your capability to achieve your goals. New leaders, like everyone else, come to each situation with their own set of preconceptions and biases. Be prepared to rebuild leadership support for your efforts at any time, whether they are new leaders, or ones you already have aligned.

Don't take leadership's support for granted once you have won it. The most successful sales people in the world never assume a client is locked in with them once they've made a sale. This will be especially true in terms of business leadership support, because the business has to react much quicker to external customers than IT does to internal customers. Never miss an opportunity to reinforce to leadership the benefits of your work, and how it supports their goals.

Almost all of the work IT does is invisible to the front-line operations. That's appropriate. IT's mission is not about technological excellence, it's about enabling the business, and the company as a whole, to be more successful. However, many ITSM initiatives make the error of failing to make their efforts, and the benefits they will deliver, more visible to the front line. They focus only on the IT management layers. Efforts not understood, are usually not appreciated. Sell front-line operations on your ITSM initiative, at least as strongly as you sell IT management.

CHAPTER 2: STRANGE BEDFELLOWS

I sat opposite Lee, as he paged through a file folder on his desk. He lingered on some of the pages, often with an accompanying "Hmm," or a disapproving shake of his head. Each time I started to say something, he held up an index finger and wagged it at me to be quiet.

He had insisted I come back and meet with him right now, but he was completely ignoring me. I wondered if this were some kind of test. But if it were, what was he looking for? Did he want to see if I would wait patiently and respectfully for him, or if I would force him to stop and pay attention?

I studied his office a little more, looking for clues. A clock hung on the wall behind his desk where only his visitors could see it, ticking loudly like the heartbeat of the room. Unlike the rest of the industrial wall clocks used throughout the building, this one looked like an antique, with an ornate Victorian wood case. It must have been expensive and meant to impress, but to me, it seemed more an affectation than a demonstration of importance. It was probably some way of him saying his time was more valuable than theirs, so they'd better be conscious of how much they used.

Finally, Lee closed the folder. Straightening his tie and picking a bit of lint from his sleeve, he cleared his throat, and flashed that Cheshire Cat smile at me.

"So Chris, you don't mind if I call you Chris, do you? Or would you prefer me to call you by your full name"? He opened the folder again and started to hunt through it.

I cut him off. "Chris is fine. Everyone calls me Chris."

"Good. It seems you have only been at the company for less than a year, so you probably haven't had the opportunity to fully appreciate how we do things. Maybe you haven't had time to pick up too many bad habits from IT here yet. Still, you probably had one or two relevant experiences elsewhere. Whether or not they are usable will remain to be seen."

Somehow, that seemed to be what Lee thought of as a compliment, so I said, "Thanks." His slight nod in response suggested I might be correct.

"I'm just a little surprised you haven't progressed further in your career by now. Don't you have any ambition? Are you lazy, or have you just reached the limits of your capability"?

I was stunned by the audacity of the question, but couldn't manage anything more cogent than, "Huh"?

"You are only a few years younger than I, but by the time I was your age, I was a senior manager, with a staff of 15 and working towards a director role in the local division. I don't expect you to be as successful as I have been, but even you must admit that rather than being a sole contributor at the bottom of the pile when any reasonably capable and motivated person would at least be in a role at your current manager's level, shows a lack of either motivation or capability on your part." Lee paused for a moment and added, "Don't you have any pride in yourself"?

Lee folded his hands together on the desk between us and sat silent, staring directly at me.

I was angered by Lee's insinuations, but sure he was looking to judge my reaction. It was the kind of thing I would expect him to do, but the why escaped me. I did not want to play whatever game Lee was pushing. Ramesh never talked about this kind of career path stuff. It was too soon. I'd just gotten here. And frankly, I didn't see a whole lot of pluses to managing teams of people and spending my time wading through an endless stream of HR paperwork.

Maybe Lee was waiting for me to scream at him so he'd have an easy reason for getting me fired. Maybe he was trying to see how hard he could push me; if I'd buckle under and go along with whatever he wanted. Maybe he wanted me to stand up and push back at him. The only thing I was sure of was that he was more interested in the lint he'd brushed off his sleeve than my career path and trying to help me.

I'd seen his type before at other companies. Lee was all about Lee and nothing else. Everyone and everything was here for him to use to advance his own interests. Everything else was unimportant. I failed to hold back a small smile.

"Did I say something funny"? asked Lee, when he spotted my grin.

"Nothing, I was just reflecting on my prior work experiences in light of your feedback."

"And your conclusion"?

"I've only been here a little while and believe that, until I know more about the company, it's premature for detailed conversations with my manager about my career path. While I appreciate your feedback ... "

"Wrong!" Lee cut me off. He stood up and walked over to the window, his back to me, and his form reduced to a shadow against the bright sunlight shining in. The brilliant light created almost a golden aura around his outline.

With his back still to me, Lee said, "You're wrong on several counts. First, it is never too early to work on your next job. Second, moving to your new job has little to do with how long you have been in your current job, and third, your career path has little to do with your current manager and what they want. You own your career path. You are the one responsible for it, regardless of who you work for. You'll work for many different people, but your career path is your bedrock."

"But how can I possibly work on it in a vacuum by myself"? I asked.

"That's why you have mentors; people who can offer wisdom based on their greater experience. They give continuity to your experience. Managers come and managers go, but your mentors are there forever. They are the ones that help you stay consistently focused, regardless of who you work for."

Lee walked around behind me. Standing over me, he placed his hands on the back of my chair.

"You see, Chris, I've accomplished more than everyone else, but I haven't done it alone. I cannot do it alone. No one can. Do you know why"?

I shook my head.

"Because there are always people who resist change, no matter how big the benefits. I am change. I am not the stone who resists the stream. I harness the stream to my purpose."

If he next asked me to snatch the pebble from his hand, I was going to break out laughing. "So what does this have to do with me and my career that you keep talking about"?

"I need people deep in the organization that trust me and work with me; people who support our goals and keep me apprised of what others are saying, so I can deal with it at my level."

"You want me to be an informer? That's how you advanced your career? You turned on your friends"?

"Not at all. You people in IT don't get it. What you do is no different from what goes on in sales or service. You just have different tools. Take away those tools and it's all about people. It's always all about people and changing their minds. That's why sales is the purest form of business. We change the way people look at things. We do it every day, and we understand it is what makes this all work. You confused people in IT still don't get it. That's why the executives can bring me back here and hold me accountable for changing IT; because it isn't about knowing the most about technology. It is about picking the right people, and getting them to work the right way. I'm looking for enlightened partners to help me educate and convince people why change makes sense.

He was getting out of his depth and it showed. He was going to fail miserably if he truly believed that. But if he didn't, what was he trying to convince me of? Or was he testing me again? "What kind of changes do you have in mind"? I asked.

"We need to change the way IT interacts with the field. When we deal with the customers … the people who give us money and keep the company in business, we don't make them deal with a dozen sales reps, each of whom has their own narrow area of specialty. We don't give them a bunch of piece-parts and expect them to figure it out. We give them a complete turn-key solution."

Lee leaned forward. "There is an old rule in sales that you should put as few barriers between people who want to give you money, and yourself, as possible. That's what sales lives by. I am going to put IT on that same footing. I am going to change the way IT works."

I shook my head. "I don't understand how it applies to IT"?

Silently, Lee walked back around and sat down at his desk.

Shaking his head, he said, "You really are dimmer than I was led to believe. Do you know how many people a sales manager has to contact, to get something as simple as a PC for a new employee"?

Lee smacked his hand down on the desk. "Eight. Eight different people, and none of them are accountable for making it happen, or knows a lot about what the others do. They just do their own little set of tasks and then toss it over the wall to the next. Why is no one accountable for the end to end resolution of that simple task? Do you know how much time is wasted … taken away from time generating revenue, to make up for IT's inability to do their job properly"?

"With all due respect, we work very hard to give the field maximum flexibility in determining which of our services they use. There are lots of different kinds of PCs people may want."

"But how many do they need? Does each sales rep, who knows less about technology than their children, need a different kind of PC, built in its own unique way, to their personal whims? No, of course not. It's just a tool. Business is not about nuances of tools. It is about people and behaviors."

Lee sat back in his chair and laughed. "IT doesn't give us services. IT gives us a box of components and we have to figure out what parts go together. IT couldn't bundle them into services if their lives depended on it. The field doesn't want a box of parts; they want solutions that help them get their job done. It's called providing a service."

"Well, how is IT supposed to know what the field operations want? We're not mind readers, you know."

Lee shook his head and slammed his folder shut. He pointed to the door. "You're hopeless. Get out of here."

I stood up and headed for the door. Just before I reached it, Lee said, "Did you ever think to ask"?

Tips that would have helped Chris

People very skilled in interpersonal interactions, may ask questions that don't make sense to you. Often, they don't really care about your answer. They are examining how you respond to the question. You will greatly increase your relationship-building strength if you look at the things a person says to you from three perspectives:

1) What is the interaction about?

2) How are they speaking about it?

3) Why are they speaking about it?

Spend time working with people outside of IT. Each group in the company has its own perspective and priorities. If you want to improve your support of other organizations, consider spending time shadowing some of their people for a day or two. Learn what their concerns are, and what they need to succeed in their terms, not yours. It can only make you better.

People will take you into their confidence for a variety of reasons. Sometimes it is to understand your true position on an issue, without revealing where they stand. Sometimes it is because they want your help, and need to give you information not available to the general population. Sometimes it is to gain your trust, because you can only gain trust by giving trust. Try to understand why a person is giving you unprecedented access, or unusually confidential information, before you sign on.

CHAPTER 3: DON'T CONFUSE ME WITH FACTS

Sunrise and Rubber Boots were the two projects being reviewed by the Project Portfolio Board today. Rubber Boots was first, with Crayton presenting Sunrise second. Project reviews were held in what was officially labeled as the "Board Room." Although, every once in a while, someone would slap a label over the sign outside the door, rewriting it as the "Bored Room."

It was about five minutes before the meeting start. Sean sat next to me. He'd been with the company in IT for his entire career, and had given me a lot of help during my work on implementing the ITSM iron triangle of incident, change and problem management. The room was packed with representatives from teams working on the projects, in one capacity or another.

As we waited for the meeting to start, Sean nudged me and snickered, "First time in the Bored Room, Chris"?

I nodded. IT humor is a strange and fearful thing to behold.

"Back in the early days, the Executives and Board of Directors actually used to meet in this room," said Sean. "That was before they got their own building and dumped this one on IT. They called it facilities recycling. We called it dumpster diving."

The room had originally been built to a higher aesthetic standard than the usual IT conference room. There were fake paneled walls that once upon a time, and under cursory inspection, might have passed for actual wood. A projector hung down from the ceiling, but the color balance circuitry had gone haywire a long time ago.

3: Don't Confuse me with Facts

We sat around an enormous wooden table, surrounded by high-backed simulated leather chairs. In its day, it was probably posh. Now, the table was scratched and scuffed. The far end of the room held an ever-growing herd of broken chairs, and I wasn't quite sure which had more dirt and stains; the walls, or the carpet on the floor.

"Where's Ramesh"? asked Sean. "He is supposed to be at all of these meetings, but I don't see him here today. Is he out sick? Or did he get some special dispensation so he doesn't have to attend anymore"?

I shook my head. "Haven't seen him, but that's not unusual, unless he wants something, or hasn't met his quota for yelling at me." I wasn't too upset about him not being there. I never could figure out why he'd hired me. Everything I did seemed to be wrong in his eyes, and it seemed like he took great pleasure in chastising me, no matter how minor the issue. I was grateful for even a small amount of time without him in my face every day correcting my work.

"He's lucky to have escaped," said Sean. "Be grateful you don't have to attend all of these meetings and suffer through the endless scuffles about which project in the portfolio is more worthy than the next. No priority, no funding. No funding, no job. Watching chair-warming project manager's fight for the survival of their cushy assignments, with lots of pay and little work, makes for entertaining theater."

Sean paused for a second, then added with a sarcastic smile, "Not you or your presentation ... I'm sure."

Sean had been attending these product portfolio meetings for years. He owned integrating new products and services into production operations once they were ready, and these meetings kept him apprised of the pipeline he faced.

"Don't they all move forward eventually"? I asked. "After all, why would we invest money in projects that made no sense"?

"Now there is your problem. You expect everything we do here to make sense."

"How many of these meetings do you attend a month"? I asked.

"I have a cot under the table. I'm thinking of carving my initials in the table to reserve my spot," he laughed. "There are a lot of in-flight project reviews each month."

"But why so many meetings? Can't we just war-room them through, and get it all done at once"?

"Trying to cover all of them in a single meeting would overload even you into stupefaction and lousy decisions. Several years ago," he pointed to the end of the table. "Sabrina, the program manager for the project management office, established this protocol, and it works well … at least most people are happy with it."

"Who's not"?

"The users, of course. Those folks sitting around on their backsides doing nothing, while we work for them, to complete the initiative. It's like they think unless they see their project getting checked every week, no one in IT is working on it."

"Why do they believe that"?

"No idea," shrugged Sean. "Maybe they slept through class the day it was explained that activity and effort are not the same. Or maybe it's just that they are users, and all users are a pain."

"But the users aren't here. Maybe that's why they're worried."

Sean shook his head. "The users are represented by the project managers. They are the voice of the customer. Most users wouldn't understand anything we're talking about. That's part of the PM's role. It's their job to get the message out to the user. It keeps users from distracting IT from its mission to get this stuff built for them. If we stopped to explain everything we do to them, we'd never get anything done. Our job is to add capabilities ... capabilities users can assemble to meet whatever need they have. That's what we do. We are a service organization, because we serve the user best by providing them with a bunch of IT capabilities."

"That's not what Lee thinks," I said. "When you deliver a service, you deliver value to your clients. Projects that produce devices and capabilities, are just tools to deliver that value. Clients don't care about the parts; they care about how it helps them meet their goals."

"Services are intangible; you don't need a project to manage putting them in place. Services are easy," said Sean. "You just lay out a process and procedure that integrates all the capabilities they need. Even a child can do that, so I know the users are capable of doing it. We shouldn't need to prioritize them. Once we deliver it, our job is done. Projects have beginnings, middles, and ends. Projects are what's important. They produce tangible things that our clients can use. A service is just a pre-structured way to respond to tasks and requests. It's a bureaucratic thing. There is nothing tangible or special about it."

Either Sean was wrong, or Lee was wrong. "Who do you think learns what these services are, and communicates them, and executes them, and improves them over time? And who in the world wants to wade through all of them to find what they want? What if a user needs something beyond what just one project can give, or a user wants something we did for another user last year"?

"When the need is there, someone will always step up for the good of the company, and make sure all the pieces get put together for whatever the users need. They don't have to be told; they don't have to have it as part of their job description; they don't even have to get credit for it. They run their shops like they were their own business and do what's right for the company once they see the need. We hire great people in IT. Give them some credit."

I shook my head. Sean had a lot more experience than I did, but I'd never seen anything before. Maybe the company did do a better job of hiring and promoting their leaders. "That sounds crazy. Why would they do that, and take on more work, for no credit, unless everyone is lying when they tell me they are overworked already"?

"You must have been listening to the new golden-boy, Lee. Did it ever occur to you he doesn't know a thing about how IT works, and perhaps even what the field really wants"?

I never got a chance to respond. From the back of the room, Sabrina, the head of the project management organization and leader of the meeting said, "Sean and Chris. If you are done having your meeting, would you mind terribly if we had ours"?

Sabrina sat in the back of the room, at the narrow end of the table. As head of the PMO, she was responsible for the entire project management function and all the project managers at the company. Sabrina was not a senior director, although by virtue of her role and reporting relationships, she was a peer of Lee in the company. In one sense, she represented the opposite of Lee. Where Lee was a lone agent with a focused deliverable, without a direct staff and tasked to succeed by influence alone, Sabrina was the head of a large organization, with many diverse deliverables, and many individuals to push them to completion.

It was her job to balance the hundreds of project requests against IT's capacity, and the available funding. That meant she said "No" a lot and made many people unhappy. But everyone in IT did agree her process was fair and nothing ever got personal.

Her process involved scoring projects on multiple attributes, from business impact to resource needs, and then putting them all through a bubble sort with the entire group to create a rank order prioritization. When the resources or capabilities for the year were exhausted, she drew a line and everything prioritized below those projects was deferred until later. When a new project came along it got ranked as more or less important than other projects, until it bubbled to its appropriate level of importance.

With a grand sweeping gesture of his hand, Sean said, "For someone as important and influential as you, Sabrina, I am powerless to resist. You may proceed with your meeting if you are ready."

While I waited for Sabrina to verbally smack down Sean, everyone else laughed and even Sabrina smiled. "Thank you, Sean. You remain the gallant gentleman as always."

Apparently Sabrina liked to keep things light and bouncy. Although it was my first meeting, I followed Sean's lead. "And you also have my permission to move forward with which must be a much more important discussion than the one Sean and I were having," I added in a theatrical voice. Except in my case no one laughed, especially Sabrina. Instead she scowled at me and made some quick notes.

Sean leaned over and with a chuckle, whispered, "Many years ago, I hired her into the company when she was fresh out of college. We've known each other for a very long time."

It was as silent as an empty room for an instant, before Sabrina said, "Let's get going, people. We have a lot of material to cover. Who's presenting Rubber Boots today"?

"That's your cue," said Sean.

I stood up and said, "I am."

I made my way to the front of the room, inserted the memory stick into a laptop connected to the projector and began with the first slide.

Lee showed up about halfway through my presentation. He opened the door without knocking and walked across the front of the room, in front of the projected image on the screen, in front of me, and sat down to my left. I stopped while he spent a few minutes noisily adjusting his chair and himself. Short of setting his hair on fire, there wasn't much more he could have done to ensure that everyone was paying attention to him and his grand entrance.

After Lee was done fidgeting, he looked at me and said, "You may continue." I finished the rest of the presentation without interruption. The one time I glanced over at him,

Lee was focused on his tablet, and I could have sworn he was watching a video.

At the conclusion, I asked, "Any questions"?

Not being familiar with the audience, I had no idea how they responded to these updates. Part of me wished Ramesh were here, so he could give me some cues, or at least see what a great job I had done on the presentation. After a few moments of silence, I assumed there were no questions.

After all the drama in his entrance, I half expected Lee to say something. I was gathering my material when Lee stood up and stepped in front of me.

"Hello. Not all of you know me yet, but I'm looking forward to knowing each of you, and having the privilege of working with you. My name is Lee. The executive leadership of this company has asked me to lend some real-world perspective to all the hard work that transpires here. Their objective is to ensure IT's efforts remain focused on helping the company continue its success, by providing field operations with the services they need to excel."

Lee put his hand on my shoulder and gave his Cheshire Cat smile to the group.

"Although members of my team are providing you with an update on this project, please understand that I am evaluating the project work to date, as well as the tasks and task owners going forward. Rubber Boots is important to the field, and I want to ensure it is properly prioritized. With everyone's support and hard work, I am sure we will make this a reference project against which future efforts are measured. I'm looking forward to working with all of you."

3: Don't Confuse me with Facts

Lee started to walk away, and then added, "Oh, and my taking over management of these, and any other projects, is not a negative reflection on anyone. If anything, it is an indication of their importance to our collective success." Lee settled back into his chair. Only then did he point to Crayton and say, "You may proceed."

Tips that would have helped Chris

The concept of a "service" is essential to ITSM. Unfortunately, it's a definition people often fight over, and even definitions from various best practices tend to vacillate over time, in the search for the best way to explain it. From a practical perspective, think of it as a bundle of IT capabilities, that when exercised, give the user a new capability they want, understand, and can directly apply in a way that improves their ability to meet their goals.

Transparency builds trust in leadership and confidence in employees. IT never has the resources to pursue all the projects requested, especially at the same time. All are great ideas, but ways must be found to prioritize. Weak leadership will often prioritize based on the volume, or frequency of protests, or personal relationships. That weakens the company and makes employees cynical and passive aggressive.

Prioritization methods need to be simple. Too often companies develop processes so convoluted and needlessly quantitative, that the assessment of the project gets less than it should. That results in people becoming incorrectly focused on the measurement tool and not the goal.

Prioritization decisions need input from everyone. Many companies make their project decisions with only people from IT in the room. Users need to have a direct part in the decision-making process. Without that, they will feel no ownership, nor any investment in the project's success.

CHAPTER 4: BLIND ME WITH SCIENCE

"Not quite yet, if you please, Crayton. First, we need to verify the current prioritization for Rubber Boots is correct," said Sabrina, as she shuffled her materials. "At the moment it is listed as project number 25. Anyone think it is less critical than the project "Open Boat," currently at number 26"?

A muddle chorus of "No" came from the attendees.

"Is it more important than project 24"?

Heads nodded. "Sure, let's move it up," said Sean. "I'd move it up over the next three projects for sure."

"Sorry, we can't," said Sabrina, as she looked through her papers. "The complete set of IT resources it requires aren't available above 23 for another three quarters. Rubber Boots will have to be at 23rd in the priority list, and remain on hold due to lack of resources for now."

"23"? asked Lee. "This is one of the top-priority field projects. It needs to be at number one."

Sabrina smiled at Lee. "I know this is your first time at a prioritization meeting, Lee. Please let me explain. We use a simple consensus bubble sort to rank the projects, and then constrain them by available resources, to get their final priority. In other words, we look at the next highest project, and see if that one is more or less important. If it is, and we have the resources available, then we move it up. Otherwise, it stays where it is, unless one below it is now more important, or needs different resources which are now available. That way the most important things get done first, and we have the maximum efficiency in resource utilization."

Sabrina sifted through her papers. "IT has determined that Rubber Boots is number three in terms of priority for the field. But it shares very scarce resources with projects of an overall higher priority that are ahead of it. The resources it needs are not available until later in the year, so it has to stay lower on the list until there are resources available. I am sorry, but better to hold off its start than assign some resources to it, and have them wastefully sit idle while other key resources are unavailable. Rubber Boots hasn't been removed, just deferred to later in the year."

Lee sat silent, glaring at Sabrina for a moment, and then said. "You cannot ignore the wishes of the executive leadership to prioritize field operations above everything else."

"We appreciate your input, Lee, there are many more factors involved here, beyond what is the most immediately important to the field. Unfortunately, IT does not have the resources available to advance every project simultaneously."

Sabrina waited for a few seconds, and then looked around the room. "In respect to everyone else's time and schedule, I'm going to move on to the next project."

Sabrina nodded, and began writing in her notebook as Crayton displayed the status summary of the project Sunrise. It was number 20 on the priority list and had been underway for quite some time.

I'd talked with Crayton after my meeting with Lee, and although he'd admitted to having a meeting with Lee, he was not very forthcoming on the specifics. I didn't really care. Probably it was something he was uncomfortable talking about, especially the way Lee laid it on thick. That's when he'd given me a preview of this presentation.

I liked Crayton's presentation. He insisted each of the project team members present to the group. Everyone gave updates on their portion of the project, as well as risks and opportunities to their deliverables. It really gave everyone a feeling of ownership. I'd have to bring my project team to the next review and do the same thing.

Lee sat back and watched it all. He never made any notes … never wrote anything down. He simply sat there; his Cheshire Cat smile replaced by a scowl, while Sabrina, on the other hand, continued to take copious notes.

"As you can see from the chart," said Crayton. "The Sunrise project is on schedule for delivery and our earned value is on target. The entire feature profile remains green, and our projected spending should bring us in at 98% of budget. Overall, commendations to the project team for executing the plan as designed. You all make this so easy."

Crayton fumbled through his notes for a moment, then asked, "Are there any questions"?

Everyone in the room sat silent. If no questions were the norm, why have these meetings? Wouldn't everyone have been better served simply by sending out an e-mail status? And why worry about someone else's project unless you needed it? Yours was the only one you got graded on. If someone else's project failed, that was their problem.

The meeting was running overtime, so without waiting for a formal close to the meeting, people started packing up their papers and filling out. Crayton looked at the procession leaving the room and said, "Well, if that's all, please keep me updated if any issues or questions arise."

Lee stood up and walked to the back of the room where Sabina sat. He sat down in the chair beside her and said, "This was our first meeting and I'm afraid we may have gotten off on the wrong foot. So I wanted to spend a few minutes with you, so my concerns are not taken the wrong way."

Sabrina checked the time and said, "Sure, but I only have a couple of minutes. I'm already due in another meeting."

"Of course," said Lee. "But given the actions of senior leadership, I'm sure you understand the top priority of projects like Rubber Boots. I want to make sure we treat it accordingly."

Sabrina shuffled her papers and stuffed them into her portfolio. "Rubber Boots will be treated according to its priority, as determined during these project planning meetings. It is in-plan for this year, but definitely not the number one project, and for now on-hold due to lack of resources."

"We need to find a way to change that," said Lee. "One of the reasons the executive team brought me back from the field, was to ensure the field gets better and faster, new services. The field sales teams need this new functionality, in order to make their numbers for the balance of the year." Lee leaned closer to Sabrina and in a quiet voice said, "You can't be telling me that you are countermanding decisions by the senior leadership. So I assume it is simply you don't understand that from the field standpoint, your prioritization mechanism is ... " he paused, "... Not viewed as a successful means of apportioning IT resources. They have told me there is no priority in this company higher than the needs of the field ... the revenue generators, and quite a few of them feel your system does not give the field projects sufficient weight."

Sabrina smiled and let out a sigh. "Lee, you don't understand. Adding new functionality is the lowest priority of any work we do."

Lee's smile dropped away. It seemed to peel away his entire slick veneer.

"Our top priority is always user-impacting events; things that directly disrupt business operations that are currently in place," said Sabrina. "Next are the projects designed to sustain the current services we provide our users. For example, there are a series of lifecycle upgrades that must take place this year, or a huge number of existing critical systems will begin to fail by the end of year. If that happens, our ability to conduct business will grind to a halt. The people needed for that are the same people needed for the Rubber Boots project, so Rubber Boots is relatively less important. Resources are always limited, and delivering new things is just not as important as ensuring that what's in place continues to run."

Lee sat back in his chair and nodded. "Have we considered some out of the box options, such as bringing on temporary workers to complete the lifecycle upgrades, so we can focus on the important projects? Or maybe we should revisit the schedule for the lifecycle upgrades, in light of the new prioritization from the executives."

Sabrina stood up and began slowly walking toward the door. "Lee, I really appreciate your fresh approach to this, but believe it or not, the PMO has been doing this for quite some time, and doing it with a great deal of success. It's a difficult job to balance delivery with available resources in the best interests of the company as a whole. I understand that your project may seem like the most important one in the list to making your quotas. However, you must understand that everyone feels that way. That's why the PMO, with its independent role, is responsible for managing those conflicting needs for the entire corporation."

Lee's tone got softer and warmer. His smile grew wider. "Sabrina, I hope you don't think my comments reflect my personal opinions. I am just a messenger. I'm not suggesting the PMO is failing its charter. Everything I've heard from people here in IT reinforces their support for what your organization has done. I'm simply providing you with some input you may not have recently heard. Rightly or wrongly, the field is complaining consistently and loudly that IT projects are being worked, instead of critical field projects. Everything we do needs to be addressed through the triple lens of input from the field: volume of complaints, consistency of complaints and intensity of the complaints."

"The field has always complained," interrupted Crayton. "If we gave them every slot and every dollar, they'd still complain."

"That's enough, Crayton," snapped Sabrina. "I do not want to hear that kind of attitude out of you ever again. Without the field we are out of business."

Crayton looked at his feet while nodding sheepishly.

"I understand Crayton's frustration," said Lee. "Unfortunately, because the field generates the revenue for the company, the executives pay very close attention to what they say, and will go to great lengths to remove any barriers, or potential excuses, as to why quarterly numbers are not met. That's why the executives brought me here from the field. I personally lose a lot of money by being here, but the field will accept my assessment of the real story of why their projects are not getting done as fast as they think they should. That's what I mean when I say that I am here to ensure projects are done in the most field-sensitive way possible and then give the straight story back to the field."

Lee sat back and smiled. "In other words, Crayton, the field doesn't trust corporate any more than you trust the field. It's like staying in a bad marriage for the sake of the children, except in this case, we're staying together for the sake of the shareholders and the profits."

"That makes sense," said Sabrina with a giggle, her entire demeanor relaxing. Her shoulders and arms slackened, her breathing slowed back down, and a smile came back on her face. You could almost see the fight or flight energy leaving her body. It was as if she had decided Lee was not an enemy and perhaps potentially an ally.

I was stunned. Lee had shifted on a dime from the fire-snorting butt-kicker, to a team-building member of management. I wasn't sure which of them was the real Lee, or if any of them were the real Lee.

"Let me suggest something that might help you," said Sabrina.

"That's great," beamed Lee as he leaned forward towards Sabrina. With that big Cheshire Cat smile, "I'm all ears."

I'd never seen him so positive and eager towards another person before. This was a side that seemed incompatible with what I knew of him.

"How about if we assemble a team to evaluate the projects being planned, worked, and completed over the last year, as well as the ones from this year that were deferred, with some explanation of our decision process," said Sabina. "It would give you something to take back to the field that would make the process more transparent. So while reasonable people could disagree on the results, everyone would concede there was fairness in the process."

"Great idea," said Lee. "Who do you think should be on it? After all, I wasn't here for the decisions and I don't know everyone as well as you."

"Well, I think that Crayton should lead. It would be educational for Chris to work with him, assuming Ramesh will let Chris spend time on it. And between the two of them, they can come up with a representative list, based on the proposals we've considered over the last year. I'll vet it, of course, to make sure there's a good representation. We can review the results together to ensure you're clear on what happened."

After a quiet moment, Lee said, "Sounds great. Don't worry about Ramesh. I'm quite confident he won't be a problem."

Sabrina opened the door and as she stepped out, turned to Lee, "And if you'd like to discuss this or anything else, I'll be happy to help you adjust to the transition from the field to corporate. Just set up some time on my calendar."

Lee stood up and said, "Thanks, I really appreciate your support," before following her out the door.

As I passed down the hall back towards my cube, I noticed Lee having a quiet conversation in the corridor with Helmut, the director of human resources. When they spotted me, they stepped into Helmut's office and closed the door. I felt a cold shiver down my spine. I knew from my previous lives that nothing good ever comes out from behind closed doors when it involves your manager and the head of HR.

Tips that would have helped Chris

IT never has the resources to pursue everything, especially at the same time. All initiatives are potentially great ideas, but ways must be found to prioritize. Poor leadership will often prioritize based on the volume, or frequency, of protests or personal relationships. That weakens the company and its capabilities, and makes employees cynical and passive aggressive when they see the process exists in name only.

Leaders rarely disagree in public, especially in front of their juniors. When they do, watch out. You might as well be in a room with two fighting elephants. You can end up being what is called collateral damage. If they don't ask you to leave, volunteer.

People are capable of using, and do use, a variety of approaches when dealing with others, in order to achieve their objectives. Never assume that people have a single style, or approach, either over time or during a particular event.

CHAPTER 5: THE JOY OF CONFLICTS

It was early in the morning as I headed to Ramesh's office for my weekly one-on-one with him. I hated these meetings. They were an opportunity for him to harangue and berate me, the depth of which depended on his mood. He was my manager and I couldn't think of a single positive thing he'd ever said to me in one of these meetings. To make matters worse, it was early in the morning, I hadn't had any coffee and I was late.

I'd sent him an e-mail last night with a summary of everything that had gone on during the project review. I figured he would be pleased that I was keeping him informed, and by sending the e-mail to him at night, implying that I was working late on company business, he'd be impressed.

I hoped that during the chastisement this week for some unwritten rule I'd broken, he'd fill me in on whether Lee and Helmut skulking about after Lee's run-in with Sabrina, had any significance. Crayton had sent me a text that evening that everyone had been looking for Sabrina all afternoon, but no one knew where she'd gone to. I wondered if Lee was bad-mouthing Sabrina to HR. I'd worked for companies before where people who fell out of favor simply disappeared and weren't talked about again.

I stopped and caught myself. I'd been listening to Ramesh too much. Ramesh had one of those really paranoid political views of companies and people in them. He was always seeing conspiracies in every corner; telling me to watch out because one day someone would stab me in the back for reasons that only made sense to them. I always thanked him for the counsel, but was pretty sure he'd been watching too much television.

At least with Lee the reprimands seemed to be about specific capabilities and deliverables, or business; nothing personal involved. Ramesh was such a jerk that it always seemed personal. Maybe there was just something personal about me he didn't like. Maybe, if I were lucky, Lee's presence might give Ramesh something else to worry about. Maybe he would back off a little bit and treat me with a little more respect.

I'd always felt that if I made a mistake, I should say to go ahead and punish me if you feel the need. Just don't ride my back every day, never letting anything go, haranguing me about every little thing, so that I'm always second-guessing myself.

I was almost to Ramesh's office when I got an urgent text from Crayton to stop and call him immediately. I stepped into an empty conference room and dialed him up.

"Did you hear about what happened"? whispered Crayton over the phone, as if he were revealing state secrets. "You remember how I told you yesterday that Sabrina had disappeared? I got it on good authority that they just fired a senior manager in our area this morning."

In the brief time I'd been here, I'd learned that the firing of anyone at the senior manager or director level was a rare occasion. No one seemed to make it to that level of the organization without being adept at deflecting ownership of failure to someone further down the organization chart. To get fired, they had to have crossed someone with major organizational pull.

Surprised someone of Crayton's experience was so wound up about this, I said, "Relax. Take a deep breath. How do you know that"?

"Okay. But one of my friends is friends with a woman who is dating one of the guys that work in security doing onboarding and offboarding; you know giving and taking away access to accounts and the buildings. It's the last thing done when you're hired and the first thing done when you're fired."

"Okay ... "

"Apparently, there was a confidential communication to his team last night at 10.45 pm, to pull the access and authorization for one of the senior managers, effective immediately. They never do that when you resign, only when you get fired."

I started thinking about Lee and Helmut talking in the hall, after Lee's confrontation with Sabrina, and wondered if Crayton had just lost his boss. "Any idea who"?

"No, they wouldn't say. Only that it is someone who's been here a long time. I wonder if they will send out a note on it"?

"Don't know, but I gotta go. I'm late for Ramesh, and if I'm late he won't be happy. Thanks for the update. Let me know if you hear any more."

Ramesh had recently hired a new administrative assistant, Joan. She wasn't new to the company, having transferred over from human resources. She knew her way around and was experienced in handling people at all levels. In theory, she was supporting Ramesh and his entire team. That's how leaders at Ramesh's level justified their admins. But in practice she was his dedicated support, and the only help we got was when we were in her good graces. I'd learned early on in my career that while it's important to make your manager happy, it's even more important to keep your manager's admin even happier.

As I reached Ramesh's office, I was a little surprised to see Joan's cube was empty. It wasn't just empty. It was vacant, as if she'd been moved. I hadn't even considered that. With the loss of a senior manager, everyone was probably going to move again. No matter where I worked, whenever there was a change in the leadership ranks, everyone got moved. Everyone's work was disrupted for a week while they shifted three rows over, for reasons only leaders with more time than work on their hands truly understood. Joan was probably the first to move, so she could plan Ramesh's move. I was not looking forward to this.

I was definitely not having a good morning, and it had barely begun. The only good news was that from the not quite closed door to Ramesh's office, I could hear multiple voices. That meant I wasn't really late, regardless of what the clock said. Rather, Ramesh was running over and that was as good as a free pass.

After a few minutes I knocked, despite the voices inside, hoping that Ramesh would simply wave me off. We could reschedule and I could get some coffee and chill out in my cube until my next meeting.

I slowly pushed the door open and stuck my head in. That was when I noticed Ramesh's nameplate was missing from the slot beside his door.

"Come in, Chris. Have a seat. I'll be with you as soon as I finish this call."

I stopped. The voice was familiar ... in all the wrong ways, and it was definitely not Ramesh.

I noticed the few items Ramesh had on the walls were gone. The bookcases were empty, and five packing boxes sat taped closed in the corner. The man sitting behind the desk was Lee. He was just finishing up a conversation on the speakerphone, to a voice I had never heard before.

My mouth dropped open. Lee hung up the phone and laughed. "Remind me to play poker with you for money some time, Chris. You can't hide your emotions any better than a two year old."

I regained some small amount of composure and managed to blurt out, "Where's Ramesh"?

Lee slowly turned in the chair, surveying the office and ignoring my question. He gestured around the room. "Do you like this office? Definitely not the quality of work space I'm accustomed to. Dark, poorly lit, with no windows, and I do so hate fluorescent lighting. Too much glare and it makes everyone look like ghouls." He rapped on the desk with his knuckles. "Crummy particle board furniture, too. But it definitely is a motivator to do better so you can get out. So perhaps there is a purpose behind such a dismal office space. Too bad some people never act on it."

Lee turned back to face me. He leaned across the desk and gestured at the chair opposite him. "Please, sit." As I sat down, he leaned back and said, "Ramesh, ah yeah. It seems that Ramesh has decided to expand his record of success through other opportunities elsewhere."

"What? Since when? Why"?

"Since this morning, about 7 am. Let's just say that it is one thing to say you are on the bus to success town. But saying it isn't enough. You also have to walk the talk. That means loyalty and confidentiality are part of the fare."

None of this made any sense. Ramesh had hired me, and although he wasn't the nicest boss I'd ever had, he'd at least been direct; which is more than some others had been. Was there a connection between what had gone on yesterday with Sabrina? I figured Lee was a petty, vindictive and compulsive jerk. But did he really have the connections to get a senior manager, a peer, fired, less than two weeks after taking over his new job? He really must be wired into executive leadership. There was no other way he could have done it.

"Ramesh got fired"? I asked.

Lee's Cheshire Cat grin grew larger. "Ever watch nature shows on TV? Ever see what happens when a new predator arrives? They disrupt the food chain for a while."

"You got him fired, didn't you? Why"? I mumbled.

"Sometimes, when people are confronted with a new reality, they choose not to participate. They choose to seek success elsewhere. When that happens, it often reinforces the organizational message that there is a new sheriff in charge and changes are coming."

Lee wasn't going to admit anything, but there was no question in my mind. He had used his influence to have Ramesh fired, mostly because it sent a message to everyone else that although he held the same rank on the organization chart, and had only been here a couple of weeks, on the power chart, the one that really mattered, he was at the executive level. Lee fired Ramesh to put fear into the hearts of his peers, and probably some directors, too.

For an instant I had an image in my mind of Lee's office, with Ramesh's head stuffed and mounted on the wall like a trophy, and spaces reserved for others alongside it.

"So does this mean I now work for you"? I asked.

"Yes … if it is okay with you. Or perhaps you'd prefer something other than the bus to success town."

Was he asking if I wanted to get fired? "Not at all. I'm with you all the way."

"Good. First, forget all of the nonsense Ramesh told you, because obviously it didn't do either of you any good. I'm going to take a chance, and allow you to accompany me to a meeting with one of our major internal users. You should consider yourself privileged at this opportunity. Think of it as my way to help you get over the loss of your former manager, because I know how well you got along and how much you loved working for him," chuckled Lee.

"Understand this," he said, "I will be running the session, and you will be there strictly as an observer. If you do anything to impact our relationship with this user, you will suffer grave consequences ... very grave consequences. Is that clear"?

I nodded. Goof up and he would fire me, too. That was pretty easy to understand. If he could kick Ramesh out, getting me fired would be easy.

"Why are we talking to the users"? I asked. "Every time we talk to a user we spend 90% of the time educating them on how IT works, and then how the technology they're asking for works. And usually what they're asking for makes no technical sense at all. It's just a waste of time."

Lee scowled at me. "When was the last time you met with a user"?

"I haven't here, but users are the same everywhere. They don't know anything. Why are we tagged with training them how technology works, so they can figure out what they want us to build for them"?

"I could take a potted plant with me to the meeting and I would probably get a more intelligent partner. Did it ever occur to you that they may actually be able to provide some input IT might find useful"?

As I opened my mouth to speak, Lee held up his palm. "Wait, don't answer that. Please try to help me believe that you are not as dumb as I fear."

"When do you want to meet with them"? I asked quietly.

Lee made a show of raising his sleeve to show off his ornate watch. It looked expensive. To my taste it was more gaudy than impressive.

"We're due there in about 20 minutes."

"What should I do during the meeting"? I asked, wanting to avoid any unwritten rules I might break.

"You're hopeless," said Lee. "A child could handle what I am asking, so even you should be able to manage it. You had better get your performance up to par, or your time here will be very brief."

"I appreciate you telling me I'm not meeting your expectations, but what should I be doing"?

"Start by figuring out what you should be doing. For this meeting, just assume this is crunch time. We're meeting with a prospect for the biggest deal in the company's history, and competition is intense. If we don't get the deal, the company will be in financial trouble, and have to fire employees to keep costs down. And we'll start with you."

I still had no idea what I was supposed to do. Lee seemed to think he was still in sales and I was a new rep. I wasn't in sales. I was in IT. We didn't do things like this in IT. Why did I have to do sales things?

Tips that would have helped Chris

Assumptions can help you move quickly, by papering over gaps, but they can also move you down the wrong path just as easily. Sometimes, people will provide you with incomplete information, hoping you will make assumptions and fill in the rest to their benefit. Sometimes it's intentional, sometimes simply because they don't know, but don't wish to be seen as uninformed.

Some people will lie to you by omission, telling you only some of the information, and not clarifying, or correcting, what you assume to be the rest. In their mind they are not lying to you, and if you persistently ask the right questions directly, they will tell you all they know. The most common use of this is in implied authority, that they represent, or have the approval, or imprimatur, of someone higher up in the organization, and for that reason, you should do what they ask. It's important for you to verify, rather than assume. Don't mindlessly fill in the blanks.

There are things you know, things you don't know, and things you don't know you don't know. Unfortunately, in the absence of accurate or complete information, people tend to fabricate what's missing ... very often inaccurately.

CHAPTER 6: MASTERS OF THE UNIVERSE

Lee pulled me aside just before we reached the user's office. All the way over he had gone on and on about whom this user was, what their organization did, and all sorts of other meaningless dribble. Who cared? We were IT. We had servers, and storage, and laptops, and other IT things. You tell us what you want, and we deliver. We made it as simple as possible for the users. Sitting around listening to customers complain was what salespeople got paid for. But not wanting to end up like Ramesh, I did a lot of nodding and agreeing, at what I hoped were all the right points.

"This is an important client for IT. The service charges to them pay a lot of IT's bills, and they use IT's tools to help them generate over 20% of corporate revenues. So we need to listen to them, and empathize with them. Never forget. Once you go into that office, you're their best friend. You will do anything to get what they need from IT."

"Except commit a major felony," I laughed.

Lee stopped and glared silently at me. For an instant I thought that he would probably be okay with that, as long as it got him the deal and he didn't get caught.

Lee took a deep breath. "You're the client's agent for change. You have to convince them you're looking out for their interests, against those geeks in IT who don't care about the business at all. And most importantly, when it comes down to choices ... and believe me it will, you are going to side with them over IT."

"But we're IT. Shouldn't we get them to understand what IT has to offer? Shouldn't we be challenging them to reassess their thinking about the situation ... prod them in a way that will meet their needs, in a way IT can deliver"?

"That's where most people misunderstand clients and sales. It's sales not because you sell them on what your team does. It's sales because you sell them on you. You give them your trust, so they will trust you. You smooth the waters, take the orders, and get out. Because once you've got their trust, they are yours to do with as you want."

"And if we do something later they don't like"?

"Don't be so negative. Our job is to get the deal, and keep the complaints about it down. Once we've got that, it's time to move on, and let operations and support worry about it. That's why they have all those people on the service desk. Got it"?

I nodded, but Lee wasn't waiting for my response. He apparently assumed my compliance, and was striding through the office door as I hurried to catch up. I glanced at the name on the door, and got only as far as "Jacob," when I saw the vice president title directly below it. I knew that name. Everyone in IT knew that name. Jacob was accustomed to chewing up IT, and Jessica, our CIO, in particular, on a regular basis. He was a monster to IT, and his basic premise was that IT was incompetent and should be outsourced.

It was going to be fun watching Lee get a beat-down from someone better than him.

The first thing I noticed was how much Jacob's room looked like Lee's; plaques, certificates and photos tiling the walls; expensive furniture placed just so, and a gorgeous view out the large windows. I knew sales did more for the company than I did, but it just felt wrong that they lived like this, while I worked in a cramped, dirty cube, and had to justify in writing every pen and pad of paper I needed. IT did so much, but always got the short end of things when it came to recognition.

I got distracted standing there, checking out Jacob's office, and suddenly realized that somehow Lee had coaxed Jacob out from behind his desk, and the two of them were sitting, not facing each other, but side by side in front of the window, almost like they were watching TV together.

From what I overheard, they were talking about doing business in Thailand, and having a friendly disagreement about whether golf at the Black Mountain Golf Course in Hua Hin was really better than at the Thai Country Club in Bangkok. I didn't play golf, but they sounded like they were equally familiar with both places. Did this mean we now had to support some site in Thailand?

As soon as I got near them, Lee placed his hand on Jacob's shoulder and said, "Jacob, I want you to meet one of the people I'm going to meld into a team that truly understands our mission from the field's perspective; a team of real rainmakers who always deliver the goods."

Jacob looked like Lee's brother from a different mother, as he stood up and extended his arm. As we shook hands, he asked, "So, Chris, tell me, which do you think is the best golf course in Thailand? We're having a little disagreement and perhaps you'd like to be the tiebreaker."

I mumbled, "Don't know. Haven't been to Thailand."

"Well you do play golf, don't you"?

I shook my head. "No. Never thought it was a sport for me. I prefer basketball or hockey. I like action." I was kind of proud of the way I'd responded. It was sure to show Jacob that I was all about making things happen and getting things done.

Jacob shook his head. "Too bad."

Lee reached over and touched Jacob's arm. "Jacob, please sit for a minute. I'd love to talk golf with you all day, but I have something serious we need to talk about."

I pulled up a chair on the other side of Lee, and slightly behind him. That meant that while they could both look out the window, I sat in the shadows. All I could see was Lee's back and Jacob's head. Behind them was a slightly faded picture on the wall, with a much younger Jacob, our CEO, and several other suits, outside Saint Basil's Cathedral in Moscow.

Lee leaned forward, and as he did, Jacob leaned in towards him, too.

Lee spoke slowly and quietly. "I want to get the benefit of your insights on how IT is supporting your goals, so I can get the services you need from the IT organization. Believe me, having been in the field until very recently, I know how pitiful the support has been from IT up till now ... despite your best efforts to get more services from them. That's why I'm here. Thanks to your voice, and others, the executive team brought me here with a mandate to give IT a kick where it counts, and finally, get some decent support and services for the field."

Jacob sat back a little. "I'm really glad to hear that, Lee. But how do you plan to do that? I'm getting hoarse from making my case and no one seems to listen."

Lee sat back and crossed his legs. He paused for a moment, straightening the crease in his pants. "Much as I suspected, there were some individuals in key roles who had never made the transition to a business-centric model. And like a clogged pipe, they were causing everything to back up and create a mess. Changes have begun and more are coming."

Jacob nodded. "So I'd heard. One of my personal pain points disappeared last night. Was that your doing"?

The big Cheshire Cat smile crept onto Lee's face. "Out of respect for the privacy of the individuals involved … "

Jacob cut him off with a laugh. "Say no more, my friend." He reached out and shook Lee's hand. "Keep up the good work."

Jacob adjusted his tie. "Lee, you've had to beat quotas, so I know you realize how critical it is to have everyone focused on success all of the time. Our job as leaders is to remove the distractions ... the irritations ... the things that keep people from having a single-minded, laser-like focus on their goals. That's what we get paid for."

Lee nodded. "And if it wasn't for us keeping the troops focused on their mission, no one, not even IT, would be employed. And do we ask for much in return"?

"I mean, how hard can it be to provide us with a simple, basic level of support"? asked Jacob, slapping the arm of his chair. "I get calls every week from the field complaining about it. I had one call last week from the director of the eastern region. She has an account rep who started over three weeks ago, who still hasn't been geared-up by IT. With our fully automated CRM cloud-based systems, that makes it nearly impossible for the rep to close, or even manage, any business. How is she supposed to hold him accountable for his goals"?

Jacob began ticking off his list of issues on his fingers. "That means no way to use e-mail, create orders, check existing customers, and all of that. They are stuck sitting in the office all day, while getting paid. The customers aren't happy, I'm not happy, and I know they're not happy, because they are losing out on their commissions."

"That's terrible," said Lee.

Jacob shook his head. "How hard can it be? Get each rep a tablet, laptop, secure remote access, cell phone, desk, badges, parking passes, and permissions to all the right databases. Get it together and on their desk the morning they start, so they can be productive from day one. I could take a child to one of the stores down the street and they could buy what was needed in a matter of minutes. Why is it so difficult"?

Jacob stood up and grabbed a large vinyl binder from his desk and held it over Lee's lap. Its cheap plastic cover seemed so out of place in his office. "One of the admins left in tears a couple of weeks ago. Apparently she tried to use this thing ... " Jacob dropped it. Lee grunted as he caught it. "... that, IT calls a catalog to get the right set-up ordered. You need a PhD in computer science to figure out what you want. It's all full of gigabytes, and RAM speeds, and pixels. Who cares? Just give us the standard kit for sales representatives. We always order the same thing. Isn't there anyone in IT smart enough to figure this out"?

Lee started leafing through it as Jacob sat down and said, "And when you try to get something new, forget it. IT has some weird way of organizing, so that their projects always get done first. It's like they don't realize where the money comes from for all of their toys. I don't mind funding their playtime, but at least have the decency of letting me have the first bite."

"I mean, if they can't figure this out, who knows what a mess they've made of the more complicated things," said Jacob.

Lee shook his head slowly from side to side as Jacob talked, interrupted only by an occasional nod of agreement. At one point, Jacob stopped for breath, and Lee quickly added, "I've experienced the same thing with my teams in the field. Seems like the only way around it is to only hire people who are already employees, and hope they bring their complete kit with them."

Lee closed the binder and handed it back to Jacob, who tossed it onto the floor at his feet. "Tell me about it. I got a firsthand look at that yesterday in Sabrina's meeting."

Jacob rolled his eyes. "So I've heard. That has to be fixed. I hope you can ... manage to make that problem go away."

Jacob leaned close to Lee and looked around the room, as if to ensure no one overheard him. In a quiet voice, he asked, "You tell me, Lee. You're working with them every day. Are people in IT really that incompetent? Should we just get rid of them all, and hire some different kind of people, or maybe even turn it over to an outside firm, who'll have some money on the line if they don't perform"?

Lee paused for a moment, as if considering the options Jacob had offered. "While there are definitely some pockets of people who think they are entitled to a job no matter how little they do, overall, I don't think that's the problem. It's not about projects, or processes, or practices. It's all about leadership, because at the end of the day, leaders are the only ones that matter. Getting workers in IT is easy. The job market is full of people looking for jobs in IT. It's finding people who can lead them, that's the problem. Without good leaders, IT people are nothing but a mob of nerds with no social skills. Of course, you'll agree that no part of the company has the quality of leadership you find in the field. But they don't have to be that level of leader. Just a little better would be a huge improvement. People only do as well as their leader's demand of them. Set low expectations for performance, and that's as well as IT people will perform."

"Well, of course," said Jacob. He smiled and sat back in his chair. "So that's why you've started cleaning house at the management level, rather than the worker level."

Lee restored his Cheshire Cat grin. "Out of respect for the privacy of all employees, I do not comment on any changes in personnel, or their roles … "

Jacob interrupted him. "Yes … yes, I know the speech. But still, starting with leadership is smart … very smart. Your field experience is showing. Cleaning up corporate is all well and good, but when can I expect to see some improvement in the field? We can't tolerate having people sitting around getting paid for doing nothing. And when we hire a consultant, it's even worse."

Lee nodded. "You're right. This is a critical issue." He turned and pointed at me. "That's why Chris has stepped up and asked for the authority and accountability for making the problem go away immediately."

Jacob looked at me and smiled. I nearly dropped my notebook. No one had said anything about this to me.

Jacob leaned over and whispered to Lee, apparently somehow thinking I couldn't hear him. "Has Chris done anything of this scale and import before"?

Lee shook his head. "Not at all. But no one is born knowing any of this. Even you and I had to learn it at some point. You remember how we spot the winners on the street don't you"?

Jacob sat back and nodded. "Real winners are those that can rise to any occasion, regardless of what they have done in the past ... that real talent can handle any situation. A true manager can manage any department, under any circumstances. Those that succeed are our winners and those that don't ... "

In unison, they said, "Are freed to increase their success with new opportunities elsewhere," and ended it with a laugh.

Jacob checked his watch. I noticed he was wearing the same expensive and ornate kind of watch Lee wore. "Look, Lee, I'd love to chat some more, but I've got a geek from finance due here in five minutes."

"Say no more," said Lee, as he and Jacob stood up. "How about I buy you a beer after work on say .... Thursday? I'd really like to get the benefit of your insight on the other pain points IT is giving you, so I can take care of them."

Jacob shook Lee's hand and nodded. "I'll have my assistant update my schedule. You're still pretty new in town, so I'll have her pick a place." Jacob chuckled, and said to Lee, "And whatever you do, don't mention to her that you're associated with new employee provisioning in any way. I've delegated management of these problems to her as a stretch assignment; strictly for her career growth you understand. And that means she is on the receiving end of the calls from the field. You should have seen her the first time she asked a regional director if he'd tried using the request system."

Lee chuckled. "I can only imagine what an introduction to the view from the field that was. Still, it is very good of you to help her with her professional growth like that. But don't worry, we'll be discreet."

Jacob turned to me and said, "Glad to know someone in IT stepped up to put their job on the line to get this fixed. Hopefully, I'll get to congratulate you on your success soon. If not, it's been nice to meet you, and I am sure you will be successful in what new opportunity you discover elsewhere."

Lee laughed, and motioned for me to follow him out the door.

I didn't know how I was going to make it happen, but I was determined not to end up like Ramesh.

Tips that would have helped Chris

Always treat your users, customers and clients with at least as much respect as you have for yourself, or would like to receive from them.

People often take ownership of things they had nothing to do with, no matter how good, or bad, they are, simply because being seen as the driving force for it, drives them closer to their goals

Doing what you think is a good job isn't always a shield against being criticized. In some organizations, success can be as simple as an announcement declaring victory. In others, it is more about the sustainability of the project after its completion. Successful people manage the expectations of the evaluators, and frame what constitutes success appropriately. Sometimes this means they established the goal as the big, flashy, more noticeable parts that the evaluators could easily scrutinize. Other times it means the detailed workings that make the work sustainable. Make sure you understand where the goal line is before you try to cross it.

CHAPTER 7: HOW HARD CAN IT BE?

As soon as Lee and I turned the hall corner, I said, "Are you sure that was a good idea? I don't know any more about the details behind provisioning new employees than you do. My hands are full with the Rubber Boots project. I won't have time for it."

Lee didn't even look at me. "You'll have plenty of time for this. I haven't told you yet, but at his request, I've given the Rubber Boots project to Crayton. He's much better suited to bringing that project in successfully. I don't know why they didn't give him the whole thing from the beginning."

"What? Crayton asked for it? But I was assigned that project by Jason himself. Are you telling me you can change his decision? Why didn't you at least ask my opinion"?

Lee stopped and scowled at me. "I am your boss. The fact that I tell you that your work has changed, should be more than sufficient. I don't appreciate being challenged by you. Do you realize that some weaker managers would consider that insubordination, and grounds for firing you on the spot"?

I bit back on my frustration and anger. "It's just that I think I could have contributed more at the meeting if I had known what you were signing me up for beforehand."

"You do not understand," said Lee. "Just because I am lenient with you, does not mean we are equals. Your job is to execute the assignments I see fit to give you. That's why I am your boss, and you work for me. Your role here was to watch and learn, not to offer your ideas, unless requested."

Lee stopped and put his hand on my shoulder. "I'm not saying you have nothing worthwhile to say. But the fact is, that most of the issues and concerns you have are things that are self-limiting and holding you back, and we need to squash those. They are things I already know, and will reinforce in you by my direction. It is part of the mentoring process. It's like exercise. It may hurt a little, but it's a good hurt, because of what you get in the long run."

It was easy for Lee to make commitments for me since it was my job he was putting on the line, not his. But what choice did I have? If he had the connections to get a respected and long-term peer, fired within two weeks of getting here, then he could probably have me out the door with just a nod and a wink.

I was determined not to end up like Ramesh. Right now, having a job was more important than my pride. I needed to turn this around. "I must give you credit at how quickly you got Jacob on your side. I was expecting a full-on beat-down."

Lee nodded his head and grunted, acting surprised I would even consider he would not be successful.

"I was a little surprised that you made IT the bad guys," I said. "There is plenty of blame to go around. All the field has to do is fill out the tickets properly, and far enough in advance. Besides, you're part of IT now, aren't you? Shouldn't you defend IT? Isn't that part of your job? Can you help me understand that"?

Lee huffed in frustration. "You have so far to go. Building links to a client is based on establishing an area of commonality ... a common experience, whether good or bad, goes a long way to building those bridges. And I'll be blunt, it doesn't matter how well, or how poor, IT is doing provisioning services. Every IT group has some service area where they could be better at focusing on the needs of the business in the field."

Lee's phone buzzed. As he answered it, he said, "Now get out of here and get to work. I want results, not a lot of chatter. Prove to me that you are worthy to work here."

"But where should I start"?

Lee covered his phone and said, "Wrong question. I expect you to tell me where you started, when you come back with some positive results. Like the Spartans used to say, "Come home with the deal, or not at all. Get to work."

I walked off, thinking that didn't sound like something the Spartans would have said, but it did sound rather hard charging. I heard Lee turn on the charm with the person on the other end of his phone conversation, like he was flipping a switch. "Hi, sorry about the disruption. I was coaching one of my less-experienced employees and they needed some extra guidance."

I walked over to Sean's cube. If anyone knew where to start, he would. He'd been here long enough, and involved in so many things, he probably had a role in implementing the whole provisioning system. He'd been a great deal of help getting me through my issues with the incident, change, and problem management processes.

Sean sat with his back to me. He had two screens lit up on his desk, and I counted two laptops and one desktop computer on his desk. He was working a tablet, as he read data off the screens. I never understood how Sean got away with it. It was against company policy for employees to have more than one working computer, yet he always seemed to have more gear than a repair depot on his desk.

I knocked on the metal strip on top of his cube wall, but he didn't respond. He had one of those fish-eye mirrors to see who was behind him, so I knew he could see me.

"Sean, I need to speak with you. I need some help."

No response, just the clacking of keys, and the gentle thump of taps on his tablet.

In the past, I might have taken his lack of response to indicate it was better not to disturb him, and come back later, but not this time. Perhaps it was Lee's influence, or maybe I was just feeling more confident in my role. I sat down in a chair behind Sean and said, "Your car is on fire in the parking lot and they are giving away hundred dollar bills in the break room."

Without missing a beat, Sean said, "Let the car burn, just be a friend and go get me enough hundreds from the break room for me to buy a new car." Sean turned around. "You've gotten awfully pushy since you started working for that bag of gas from the field, Lee."

I leaned across the desk. "I would be careful what I said about Lee. Did you know he got Ramesh set free to pursue more success elsewhere"?

Sean scowled. "Don't give me that corporate double-talk. It's not even a good euphemism. I'll bet you don't even know why they fired him, do you"?

"No one ever talks about that. It's out of respect for the individual's privacy."

Sean rolled his eyes. "Give me a break. And here I thought you actually had a clue. Do you really think the leadership cares about any privacy besides their own? They want to keep the reason a mystery from those remaining behind; to keep them guessing what unwritten rule the recently departed had violated; to keep the survivors always second-guessing their actions, and working to err on the side of caution, rather than confrontation with the dictates of the leadership."

"You're crazy," I said. Now he was starting to talk like Ramesh. "There may be some strange characters in the leadership, but no more than anywhere else in the company. There is no way they could benefit from not being transparent."

Sean laughed. "By keeping information from workers, it is easier to keep them under control, and focused on their tasks. Our leadership is a group of ultra-competitive, high-performing super achievers. Their real objective is collecting more relative power than their peers. Being able to do that well, was how they got to where they are. But having spent so much time focusing on that skill, they're no longer comfortable doing anything else."

"The only way to measure their performance against their peers is through relative power. And information is the currency of power in corporations. So while leading the company is their role, it is only a means to the end. Their real objective is showing their leaders that they have accumulated more power through their actions than their peers. That is the goal of our leadership."

"You've had too much coffee and need to get out among real people more often. Or at least keep your soapbox in check."

"Fine. Ignore what I've learned. Why are you disturbing me"?

"Where should I start? Who can help me understand what's going on with provisioning technology equipment for new employees? You've been here a long time. You must know who owns that service. I've been through the organization charts, and I can't find any group, much less any person, responsible for it."

Sean seemed a little perplexed by the question. Actually, it was the first time I'd asked him a question, and not received an immediate flip answer. The fact that he wasn't making fun of my question had me worried.

"Depends on what you mean by provisioning. It's not a simple answer. There's a computer, phone, physical access, secure remote access, secure local access, domain assignment, applications; the list just keeps going. You're going to have to talk to each of the groups."

"That makes no sense. Who's accountable if it goes wrong? Who gets their performance measured, and gets rewarded if it gets better"?

"When you find them, let me know. I have a few other miracles I need worked," he laughed. "Do you seriously think that IT is so overstaffed we can dedicate people to doing nothing more than watching to see if other IT groups are working in concert with each other? And don't forget, IT doesn't even own a lot of the tasks you're talking about. Keep this up and I'll begin to think you're really Lee in disguise. We have a lot of smart, responsible leaders in IT ... people who have the users' best interests at heart. And when people involved in provisioning new employees get task requests, you can be sure that one of them will step up

... even though it is outside their area of expertise ... and make sure the work gets done end to end. That's how we provide service to the business and leverage them for success."

At least he was making fun of my questions again, but if his comments were true, they were a big reason for the gaps in delivery. The only question was how to fix it, because he was absolutely right. IT could never get dedicated bodies to manage it, and if no one was held accountable for it, then things could go wrong and never get addressed ... or even done the same way twice.

"You still here"? asked Sean with a smile. "I suppose you won't leave my cube until I tell you where to go. Okay, start with Ian. He's in charge of asset management. He has to track everything for the accountants, so he should be able to at least tell you who has which piece. Now go away. I have real work to do."

I headed down the main isle of the cube farm towards Ian's office. As owner of asset management, he could tell me which assets were given to which employees, and that would provide me with a pattern for how things were being handled. I'd arranged for us to have lunch off-site, so I could have some time picking his brain without interruptions.

Part of me was hoping that he was also responsible for ensuring no tools were left with departing employees, and that their access was cut off the day they left. Usually things went well, although there had been a couple of incidents where employee access had been cut off by Ian's overzealous staff before the employee even knew they were being let go. It was a miserable way to find out you were being fired. I bet Lee and Jacob hadn't even thought of that final humiliation for the soon departing.

I walked quickly. The idea of knowing something Sean didn't, and being able to rub his nose in it, was very appealing. And as Jacob and Lee had insisted, there was no sense in having employees here if they didn't have the tools they needed to do their job. I was more than a little surprised that I was actually starting to enjoy this assignment.

Ian and his team sat in an area of cubicles that were former raised floor data centre space. It had been converted into a cube farm, by simply laying down some carpet, and adding cubes. The raised floor was still in place, even after all the cabling had been removed, leaving the plenum as an empty, resonating cavern, much like the box of an acoustic speaker. In a few spots, orange safety cones identified the booby traps of broken floor panels that hadn't yet been repaired. Judging by the dust on them, they weren't likely to be repaired anytime soon.

I turned into Ian's cube and almost ran down Zoey. She was the new administrative assistant for Jason, our Senior VP of sales and marketing. Zoey was peppering Ian with questions in a non-stop flow that made them nearly rhetorical. She didn't seem very interested in answers, only demands.

"Where are the systems for our new hires," demanded Zoey, stomping a foot against the floor, hard enough to make it echo.

"How hard can it be"? she demanded. "These are 12 new sales associates. They each need a smart phone, tablet and laptop." She gestured across Ian's cube. "They don't need much, because unlike some employees, they are out in the field actually generating revenue, so you can sit in here on your rear every day."

Ian began to sift through the online equipment request data. "Just a minute, let me check."

"You're just checking now! These requests were loaded weeks ago." Zoey waived a sheaf of papers at him. "My boss thinks I goofed up and forgot it. I am not going to take the fall for your failure."

"Look, I'll be happy to talk to him and explain the circumstances," offered Ian. "Just let me get the dates and times, and estimated completions, first. I'm doing this as a favor to you. I'm not accountable for new employee gear you know."

I shook my head. That was not the situation I'd hoped for.

"Do you think he is any more interested in excuses than I am"? She slapped her hands down on Ian's desk, and loomed over it towards him. "I want that technology in place today, and if not, there will be repercussions you will not like."

With that, she turned around so hard I thought she'd get whiplash. "Excuse me," she snarled, shoving past me and into the hall.

I smiled at Ian and said, "Glad you're having fun."

Ian glared at me. "This is insane. Can we go to lunch now, before someone else comes to beat me up"?

We walked quickly toward the parking lot. Ian seemed to check each row before we crossed, as if he were looking to ensure no one else was waiting to ambush him. We were only a couple of rows from the door when Ian finally relaxed a little.

"You don't have anything like this," he said. "Every flipping request seems to work differently. I get one kind of form from some people for new employee set-up. Then I get requests from the service desk for a set-up, but no one seems to know if it is the same one or not. Then I get people like Zoey, cube-bombing me with more demands. Half of them are so detailed I doubt anyone outside of IT could fill them out, and the rest are so vague that no one could figure out what was really needed. And the worst part is, they are all probably for the same people, and most don't make any sense."

"Well, who is supposed to feed you those requests"? I asked. "Somebody must own this. Who's accountable"?

Before he could respond, Adrianna came running up behind us. "Just the person I was looking for. Where are we on those set-ups for the new employees? Are they ready yet"?

Tips that would have helped Chris

Don't be surprised if you encounter processes or procedures that have been established with great rigor, but without follow-up performance goals in the future. People may take a project view of processes, with the deliverable being the initiation of the process, rather than its ongoing performance.

During development, and even operation of any process, you will become involved in situations that are frustrating, or upset you. Try not to let anger or frustrations drive your actions, you will regret later. Try to take a step back and focus on making fact-based decisions. When people you are working with fall into this trap, do what you can to help lead them back to the facts. Once they get there, they will thank you.

When developing new process, or analyzing existing, you will often need to hunt down connections and data flows. Don't be shy about following the dots and asking for help and directions from each person you encounter. You will usually end up with a number of dead ends, but those are valuable, too. They help you eliminate areas not worth further investigation.

CHAPTER 8: CHOW FUN

All the way to the restaurant, Ian kept up a steady patter, alternating between complaints and curses about the situation, broken only by fist shaking and yelling at other drivers. It was a good thing I was driving, and we were getting away from the office, because by the time we reached the restaurant, Ian was ready to explode.

"Why is this my flipping problem? I'm not accountable for building somebody's PC, or installing their phone. I just keep track of the stuff we buy. Just because the company is too cheap to put someone in charge of this, why does it become my problem? Why is it whenever I try to do the right thing, someone starts to beat on me? I know I'm gonna get fired over it. And it'll be for something that I'm not even accountable for. How's that for irony of Shakespearean proportions"?

"Well if not you, then who"? I asked. That was a mistake. I thought he was going to either hit me, or punch out a window.

"No, it's why me. Nobody owns IT's provisioning services for new employees. Just like nobody owns any of IT's services. I guess that way, when it gets messed up, there is no one who gets dinged for it."

It hadn't been that long since orientation. I still remembered the module on what made our IT organization better than most. "But that's because our organizational model says that if you have most of the content for a user request, then you take the lead. You step up and do it because it's for the good of all. That's what makes our IT better than most others. We all are accountable to the client and each other."

"I see you still remember your orientation class. Let me clue you in on the reality. People don't step up, because they are already overcommitted in their current assignments. Since no one owns overall responsibility, any time they invest in being accountable for these requests, just increases their risk of failure elsewhere. When everyone is accountable, no one is accountable."

I stopped adding fuel to Ian's rants. He was beyond rationality, and into the pain of his situation. I let him rage and vent while we traveled into a run-down section of the city, and pulled into the pot-holed parking lot of a small and shabby strip mall. Many of the storefronts were vacant; their windows plastered with "For Rent" signs. Our destination was a Chinese restaurant. It was bracketed by a liquor store on one side, and an adult novelties shop on the other. In front of the restaurant, the lot was crowded with parked cars. The windows of the restaurant were steamed opaque.

As we got out, Ian pointed to a sign in the window, and asked, "What the heck is Yum Cha? Is that what we're having? I don't want any of that phony fast food stuff masquerading as real Chinese food, like they eat in China. Just get me an order of General Tso's chicken and some Crab Rangoon. Give me the authentic stuff and I'm good."

I shook my head. "Yum Cha is a style, not a dish. This is a Dim Sum teahouse. You'll get to sample a lot of dishes, including my favorite, Dry-Fried Beef Chow Fun; beef, noodles, onions and sprouts. It's a test for the skill of any chef that offers it. There are a lot more ways to do it wrong than right, and it takes a true master to consistently get it right. Kind of like what you do at work."

"I doubt that. It sounds so simple even a child could do it. I don't see how that could be much of a test. Not like those idiots back in the office."

As I guided Ian into the restaurant, I said, "Hey, don't let them beat you by remote control. You're out of the office and on Ian time now. Let it go for a few minutes. Let's just have lunch and enjoy the experience." There was no way I would get anything intelligible out of him until he relaxed a little.

We worked our way over to a table, and were swamped by the sensory overload. The smell of so many different foods, mixed with the hustle of the servers, the clanging of dirty dishes being cleared from tables, and the constant buzz of conversations in so many languages, brought Ian's rant to a halt. At least this new experience would force him to think about something else for an hour, besides how much he hated his job.

But I kept thinking about what Ian had said; about how it was so simple a child could do it; simple, yet difficult. Perhaps it was the simple things, the things most visible to the business; the things they viewed as simple, no matter whether they were or not, that were the hardest of all things to consistently do right.

When we finished lunch, our table was littered with over a dozen small empty plates and bowls. I started stacking them up for fun, and they seemed to come in four basic sizes. I signaled one of the assistant managers, who came to the table and totaled up our bill. He counted the number of dishes by size with his pen, and then quickly wrote the total on the bill. Ian grabbed the bill from his hand.

"That's amazing. How do you remember the price of all those dishes, and then add them up so fast? I never even saw a menu. If you're that good with memorization and figures, you shouldn't be stuck here in this restaurant. We could use you at work."

He smiled, and in heavily accented English, said, "That is a very generous offer, Sir. But you overestimate me. Food is priced by size of the dish, we adjust the contents to provide a consistent and easy to understand price for our customers. We make it so easy, even a child could calculate the bill. Customers are the most important people in our lives. Without them, we would have nothing. And as for your very kind offer to work with you, I am afraid I must decline. My father, the owner, would not approve, and I suspect it would not match my disposition. But thank you, and I hope you have a very nice day."

I plucked the bill from Ian's hand and said, "I got it. Meet you outside."

Ian was a different man on the way back to work. He had calmed down a lot. I ascribed it to the excellent Beef Chow Fun, but the beer he had with it probably didn't hurt. No matter which, unwinding is better than stroking out.

When I dropped Ian back at the office, he pointed me straight at the service desk, for the solution to my problem. I'd always called it the help desk, but Ian had corrected me, since not only did they help you out when you had a problem, but they also were the one-stop entry point for whatever you needed to do your job. It bothered me that it was so hard to find a solution to such a simple activity that we did all the time, and that no one seemed to be responsible for it.

Ian even gave me the personal cell phone number of Manuel, the senior manager in charge of their day-to-day operations. The service desk team was housed in its own building, along with the telemarketing team. I'd called Manuel from my car phone, and followed Lee's advice, by letting him believe that I was looking for him under Jacob and Jason's direction, in order to get an immediate meeting with him.

I drove past the building without realizing it the first time. The two-story nondescript building looked like thousands of other modern office-park boxes, built to maximize internal space and minimize cost. Externally, there was no signage, or any other indicators it was a part of the company. The only clue it was occupied, was the full parking lot. Even though I had my ID pass, I still had to sign in as a guest at reception, and wait for an escort. It seemed they wouldn't let just anyone, even employees from other parts of the company, near the service desk or telemarketing team. It made some sense in that their work was so very different from the other people at headquarters. They were a production shop, just like they wouldn't let just anyone onto a manufacturing floor. It was their job to process calls, and anything that distracted them from that was bad. Their mission was to serve the customer. At least that's what I remembered from my new employee orientation.

A few minutes after I'd signed in with security and added the guest badge to my jacket, the locked door behind the security guard opened, and a smiling man, with an outstretched hand, walked through.

"You must be Chris. I'm Manuel. My team runs the service desk."

After a short, limp, handshake, he turned and headed back through the door. "Follow me."

We walked quickly along the edge of an enormous cube farm. Modern building techniques had allowed construction of the space, with no internal pillars blocking the view. The expanse was crammed with small cubes, barely big enough for a desk, chair and cabinet. Most were occupied by people wearing headsets and all talking at once. These were low-wall cubes, without even a pretense of privacy. Walls were just four feet high, slightly concealing the sitting occupants from their neighbors. On the far wall was an enormous monitor visible from every cube. It gave real-time updates in charts, the number of calls in queue, abandoned call rates, average call time, and a number of other real-time key performance indicators for the day, the week, and the month. Other monitors provided muted weather and news events in closed caption streams, crawling along the bottom of the images.

The din from the multitude of simultaneous conversations was stifling. I was grateful for the quiet when we stepped inside Manuel's heavily soundproofed office, and he closed the door. One wall of Manuel's office was glass, giving him an unrestricted view of the nodding heads and flashing screens. Behind his desk was a console with headset, that allowed him to listen in on any conversation being conducted by his team.

Opposite his desk, a large monitor hung on the wall, giving real-time updates in charts, numbers of the number of calls in queue, abandoned call rates, average call time, and a number of other key performance indicators for the day, the week and the month. It was identical to the ones installed around the walls of the cube farm, where only technicians could see them.

"This is but one site of our service desk organization," said Manuel proudly, as he gestured through the glass window of his office, over the sea of low-walled cubicles. "We are a global company, and our service desk functionality follows the sun. No matter where you are, when you reach out, we will be there for you."

"So there are no multiple shifts at this site? This space is quiet and dark for two-thirds of every day"? I asked. "Doesn't that waste a large segment of this location's capability"?

"Obviously, you don't understand the reason a service desk must follow the sun," he shot back. "I played a key role in the development and transition from our old centralized model, to this new, more responsive, model. After all, we are here to serve the users, and must arrange ourselves to accommodate them, not make our life easier. Trust me; this is the best configuration for the corporation and its customers. Many smart people were involved in this decision and I am sure it is correct."

Manuel gestured to a chair in front of his desk, and only when I was seated, did he sit down behind his desk. After shifting some papers between piles on his desk and closing a few folders, he said, "You know, Chris, we're the primary mode of contact for our customers and employees. We work very closely with our partners on the marketing and sales teams, but did you know, customers spend more time with my team than they do with anyone else? We don't get many disruptions here and rarely allow visitors, although I am always eager to hear from my leadership partners in the business. What can I do for Jacob and Jason"?

Lee had been right about that one. Just hinting at Jacob's and Jason's involvement, without even saying they were involved, was enough to get the VIP treatment; nothing like a warm welcome to make you feel at home. "Are you aware of the crisis we have in getting new employees properly equipped in the field? It seems that IT is incapable of gearing-up people to the point they can do their job with the consistency and quality the business expects."

Manuel entered some data on his computer and then gave me a look of confusion. "While I recognize you are here representing business interests." He pointed at his computer screen. "That's an interesting comment to hear from an IT person. According to my information, you are officially part of the IT organization. It is rare ... perhaps one might even say refreshingly rare, to hear someone criticize the performance of their own organization."

"Why do you say that"?

"For starters, most of the people and tasks involved in enabling new employees are in IT. It is not often I hear a function criticize itself. But more importantly, we are here to serve everyone in the company. We don't point fingers because something isn't perfect. We just try to help people get what they need, using the systems that are in place at the time. We work with the resources the company is able to provide for us, because those resources have been allocated in a way best suited to the advancement of the company as a whole."

And that's why Lee would call you all a bunch of losers, I thought. You took what was given to you and never pushed back.

"One of the keys to success is to have a single point of contact for users," he said. "It is imperative that everyone reach out to a single point. We need to be able to gather data on who is calling, and about what, so we can continually improve the services we deliver to our users. That's our job. We are the single point of contact for all services in the company. That's why they call us the service desk," said Manuel in a decidedly condescending tone, as if that should be obvious to the simplest of minds.

"Of course you are," I said. "But I have seen what Ian is going through with asset management. Users have the option of using the service desk to request services, but they also have the option of multiple other ways, too, and they seem to use all of them to get what they want."

"That's incorrect," said Manuel. "All, and I repeat, all service requests are required to go through the service desk. It is part of our charter. Other requests are invalid and ignored. While equipping new users is not officially a service. It is actually a task that draws on several services; we don't correct our users who may use the words incorrectly."

Now I was confused. I'd been told that provisioning new users was a service IT performed, not a bunch of services bundled into a task. That didn't even make any sense. That is not what I was told. I filed that away to investigate later because it seemed unimportant, just a semantics question that Lee would be upset if I spent any time on. But he would really like the idea of taking the order from the user and getting on with it. That was real customer-focused behavior.

Manuel turned and pointed to a poster on the wall that said, "The service desk is committed to building a high-performing, customer-focused team, dedicated to driving business success, user satisfaction and employee professional growth, through the creation and operation of a one-stop location for the fulfillment of requests, issue resolution, question response, and communication for all user needs, in a way that is ecologically green, and provides sustained first contact resolution and maximum efficiency of the resources the corporation provides in a continuous improvement mode."

Manuel turned back and said, "Corporate leadership has reviewed and approved that charter for the service desk. I know. I was there when they gave the go-ahead. There are no other ways to request new employee provisioning, other than the service desk. We don't perform the work ourselves, but we do assign it. And we assign tasks correctly to each of the relevant services. I have metrics to prove it. Over 99% of properly configured tasks submitted during specified working hours, through correct channels, are assigned and accepted. If Ian is handling requests through some back channels, then he is violating corporate guidelines, and should re-read the appropriate policy and process documentation."

"But what about situations where the service desk can't address it, or doesn't work fast enough, or the request is incomplete or incomprehensible"?

"I wouldn't worry. Other members of the corporate team have been instructed to refuse to process any user requests unless they follow the proper procedure, and submit them appropriately to my team for routing. You shouldn't have any problems. Anything we receive from other IT teams that does not conform to our standards represents a breakdown in their behavior. The service desk remains properly aligned with corporate process and procedure."

"What if they don't know the proper process? Isn't that kind of anti-user"?

"You've got it backwards, Chris. Users need to understand that we can serve them most efficiently if they simply follow the process and procedures. If they don't do that, because they think they're special, then they just have to understand these rules are there for their own good. If they do it right the first time, they will have it sooner."

"So you mean Ian is creating his own problem by not rejecting user requests unless they come from your team"?

"That's right. He's only hurting himself," said Manuel. "My team solves most issues on first contact. If Ian would only follow the procedures I've lain down, he would notice a drop in his volume of work, and ultimately a happier and more productive user base."

That was a relief to hear and I was sure Ian would be pleased to know there was a way to reduce his workload, too.

I nodded in agreement. "I think we can both agree that for something so essential to the business, and so simple, we need to perform flawlessly. That's where I'd like to help."

Manuel looked askance at me. "I'm not sure what you mean. Our KPIs are exactly aligned with our commitments. We are delivering as required. Isn't this a conversation you should be having with the rest of the people involved, instead of the service desk; perhaps with your associate, Ian"?

I shook my head. "Manuel, it's not about any defects or failings by your team. We need to ensure the implementation of the provisioning services is not only on target, but is optimized to get the maximum business benefit. So while that may not mean you're doing something wrong, it may mean that given how other groups interface with you, there may be opportunities for you to help them. And I know that given the service desk's commitment to our collective success, you will want to do what you can to help other teams that aren't so proficient and well managed."

I smiled on the inside. If only Lee could have heard that. It was exactly the kind of pandering ego stroking he seemed to use so successfully to get what he wanted.

"A noble sentiment," said Manuel. "However, any true leader of a function would no more welcome my critiquing their methods of operating any more than I would. It is not our business model. If each of us makes our area the best in class, then the company as a whole becomes best in class. It is so simple and obvious even a child could understand it."

That sounded like what Ian had been complaining about; that no one had end to end accountability for anything ... kind of like an orchestra without a conductor. I was about to say something when I remembered what Lee had said about how one of the reasons people fail when convincing others what to do, is that they keep selling after they get agreement. One of the hardest things in sales is knowing when to stop selling and get to inking the deal.

"Of course," I said. "Can you show me how things work; maybe let me sit in on a call or two? I'd really like to get a sense for how it feels on the front line and include that in my report. If there are any barriers your representatives are encountering in getting employees provisioned promptly, I may be able to get senior leadership to remove them for you."

"I like the sound of that," said Manuel. "Just extend me the courtesy of sharing any findings with me before you give them to management. I don't want any inaccurate information to cause undue concern among our leaders. I can help you ensure all of your salient points are correct and properly aligned."

This guy was slicker than Lee when it came to obscuring the facts. I smiled and said, "Would you? That would be an enormous help."

"Of course." Manuel checked his tablet and said, "Kourosh is working today. He is an experienced and trained representative. He will be able to handle the contacts and explain them at the same time." Manuel gestured to me as he reached for the door. "Follow me, please."

Tips that would have helped Chris

Things that appear simple are often the hardest ones to get right when managing a process. Top professionals make it look effortless; until you understand the amount of hours they've spent making it look like that. Great concepts and solutions usually seem quite simple when explained by a person who is a master at them. When assessing or designing processes, always look extra thoroughly at things that appear simple, especially if people are involved. There is a good chance it is much more complicated under the surface.

Metrics can make any organization look good or bad, independent of how effective they actually are. It is all in what is measured, how it is measured, and over what intervals. If someone's key performance indicators (KPIs) are all green and acceptable, be suspicious – especially if there seem to be operational problems. Remember the phrase, "There are three kinds of lies: lies, damned lies, and statistics."

What your clients see as the simplest tasks are the ones where they will set the highest standard for consistent successful delivery. That's because if people see them as trivial, the kind of thing they could do, then any shortfall on your part will lead them to believe that they could do a better job than you.

CHAPTER 9: HELP I NEED SOMETHING

As soon as Manuel opened the door, the chatter of the cube farm hit like heavy surf. It was mind numbing. I didn't see how the analysts could ignore it. Snippets from a river of conversations on a dozen different subjects, all overlapped in a cacophony of confusion.

We turned the corner to Kourosh's cube just as he was finishing a call. Somehow, he must have sensed our approach, because as soon as he disconnected the call, he unclipped his headset, spun around in his chair, and stood up with his hand outstretched towards me.

He looked Persian, and I expected heavily Farsi-accented English, but in the most neutral English he said, "Hello, my name is Kourosh. How may I help you"?

I laughed at my ignorance. "How did you hear us coming over all the noise"?

"It's disrupting only to the uninitiated. Once you work in it for a while, it becomes only background noise, like the hum of an air conditioner."

"And of course those that can't make that adjustment either go crazy or quit," added Manuel with a laugh.

"So, Kourosh," asked Manuel. "Chris wants to sit in on some calls and ask you some questions; get a sense for what it is like to work here."

Kourosh turned to me and smiled, "Ah, so you are thinking about joining our team? We can always use more help."

I shook my head. "No, I'm here at the request of Jacob and Jason to understand why IT is so incompetent when it comes to provisioning new employees. I thought it best to start at the beginning; the service desk, where everything begins."

"Thank you very much for the compliment," said Kourosh, "But most of the user requests can be accommodated via automated user self-service. It gives users more control over their costs, and ensures they have the utility they need."

"Does it follow a different route"? I asked. "Not really," offered Kourosh. "It just skips the service desk, and is automatically routed straight into the appropriate IT queue by software implementations of the same rules of assignment we follow."

Manuel's cell phone buzzed, and after a few words of conversation, he paused and muted the phone, saying, "I'm going to leave the two of you for a while." He looked at me and said, "Kourosh will take care of you. If you need anything else, just shout."

I wasn't sure if that was a joke, or a subtle message to not bother him again. It didn't matter. Like Lee said, I didn't care what he wanted. What mattered was my goal.

I pulled Manuel aside, tried to whisper, and ended up nearly shouting over the noise, "I hate to admit that I'm surprised Kourosh's English is better than mine."

Manuel laughed. "As is his French, Spanish, Farsi and Arabic. It's something I look for during interviews. I can teach anyone technology fairly quickly, but I cannot teach them superior language skills in a short amount of time. And to teach them customer focus can take a lifetime.

Successful hiring in the service desk business is all about knowing the difference between what can quickly be taught, and what's better if the candidates bring it with them.

I started to say, "Thanks," but Manuel had already turned his back to me and was quick-walking back down the main isle of the cube-farm.

"We should get you hooked up," said Kourosh, as he pulled a wireless headset from a desk drawer. "This is a training headset. Your microphone won't work, but you will be able to hear both sides of the conversation; everything I hear and say as well as everything the caller says. It will be just like you were taking the call."

I slipped the headset on, and found the quiet from its noise-canceling circuitry very comforting.

Kourosh's smooth voice echoed through the headset. "Can you hear me okay"?

I nodded. "So clear it is just like you were sitting next to me," I joked, and then pulled the earphone away from my head for a moment, to remind myself of the difference.

Kourosh made a few adjustments to the controls on his communication link and pointed to the large monitor on the far wall. "We've got to get busy. Wait times are creeping up over the goal levels and the call abandon rate is climbing rapidly. Our active staff is down 10% due to normal absences, and we're still down 15% on our base staff levels because recruiting can't even figure out how to hire people. And that makes no sense to me given the economy. They ought to have people lined up and ready to go in queue. They know what our turnover rates are. They should never stop making job offers, but because of an unthinking corporate policy they won't look for replacements until people have already left and we are shorthanded."

"Wait a minute; are you always this short staffed"?

"Service desk is a high turnover operation. Not many stay as long as I have. It's a very flat organization, so there isn't a lot of room for advancement. But in this company, it's always easier to transfer internally to get a job, than applying for one from the outside. The service desk is a great way to get into the company, and, after a year or so, move on to your desired job."

"Doesn't that mean you have to repeat a lot of training to keep the new people up to date"?

"Training takes time, and classroom training never substitutes for real experience. We do a lot of learning from people who are experienced, and can give you real-world knowledge. They also help close the gap between classroom training and reality."

"So you're used to taking rookies out on calls like this," I said.

Kourosh nodded, and then punched us up, and a timer began tracking on his monitor screen. A voice rang through my headset.

A woman began yelling. "I've been on hold for almost 10 minutes listening to your flipping, distorted mood music, while you were all hanging around drinking coffee and telling jokes. I've got a real problem here and I need it dealt with now."

"Hello, my name is Kourosh," said Kourosh. "Thank you for calling the service desk. I apologize for your wait time. How many I help you"?

"Well, listen up head-loose, or whatever your name is. How stupid are you that you couldn't come up with a better artificial name to hide behind; like Bob, or Jack, or Bill? My name is Jackie. I'm in the central region. One of my users created a service request nearly four weeks ago, for the creation of six, new user accounts in support of their sales staff. So far the accounts have not been created. They think I goofed up, and am responsible for it not happening. And I am not going to take the fall for your incompetence. To make matters worse, I log on to check the status, and find the ticket has been closed as completed successfully. Here's the ticket number."

"I'm very sorry you're having a problem. Let me check that for you. Will you please hold for a moment"?

"Why not? I've gotten quite used to sitting here doing nothing while waiting for you. Just don't put that awful music back on."

"No problem."

Kourosh scrolled through the list of tickets. It was huge, and a lot of them seemed to go back quite a long period of time. He had four different databases open on his screen, and was trying to manually scan through them looking for the ticket. There didn't seem to be any easy way to sort them, or order by date, in any of the applications, much less correlate the different databases.

While he worked we could hear Jackie in the background. She didn't realize that being on hold for the service desk simply meant that she was on mute.

"Here it is," said Kourosh to me, while Jackie remained on mute. "It was entered into the automated system by Jackson four weeks ago, and sent to Peter's queue over in IT's desktop support team. Problem is, I know that Peter quit about three weeks ago. Worse, it looks like Peter closed all of his open tickets as completed the day before he left. I'd guess a lot of them weren't really done. No wonder the work wasn't finished."

"So what do you tell Jackie"?

"I tell her where to go," laughed Kourosh. "Seriously, I give her the name of the manager for the desktop support team, and tell her to reach out to them, to find out how to get it handled."

I wondered how Lee would think of that. Getting bounced around seemed to be exactly the kind of thing that the field was protesting about. "Doesn't sound very customer focused," I said.

"No, it is totally customer focused. It removes the barriers, and empowers her to drive her own solution at a pace that aligns with her needs. It puts her in control of her destiny, and gives her full transparency as to what's happening. Plus it allows us to serve more users with a given amount of resources, thus helping drive the company's success."

"And it gives us all good reviews, by keeping the time on call and queues at the service desk down, because that's what we get measured on. It's important to remember that leadership has identified the measures they feel best identify the value-add of the service desk. They identify those KPIs and we drive to them. It's not my place to tell senior leadership what's important to the success of the company. I am merely the instrument of their direction."

"Hi, this is Kourosh. I apologize for keeping you on hold for so long, but I did locate that ticket. That ticket had already been closed as completed successfully."

"That's what I just told you," she screamed loud enough to hurt my ears. "That ticket was never closed. The work was never completed. I'm the one that opened the ticket. I should know."

"I appreciate that," said Kourosh. "But according to our records, our automated system contacted you after completion, and you responded to our performance survey by giving the service desk high ratings for their actions."

"Either you have the wrong ticket, or there is a forgery going on. The work is still not completed. So how do we get this fixed immediately? Can't you do it from there? It shouldn't take more than five minutes. And then I will give you my real rating of the service desk."

"We are not staffed to make changes to access or user accounts. The security group within desktop support handles all of those items ... to protect the company of course. I'm sure you understand."

Kourosh took a moment to check out his on-call time. It was creeping towards yellow, and from there it was only a short distance into a service level breach.

"I'm sure you can appreciate the need to restrict access to the tools that control access to our key systems," he said. "We will get it taken care of for you, Jackie. I just need to ensure that it gets assigned to the person best able to solve the problem for you, as quickly as possible."

"So, you're telling me you're not authorized to do it. You're too junior or unskilled to be permitted to do it, right? I want a supervisor and I want them now."

The conversation got worse from there. Kourosh never lost his calm demeanor, regardless of the taunts Jackson threw at him. He never once rose to the bait and struck back at Jackson. The only thing that seemed to give him pause was when the call timer on his screen changed to yellow and then started toward red.

Just before the clock numerals shifted from yellow to red, Kourosh passed the call off to the desktop support team.

With the caller gone, he said, "That was close. I almost got a red call."

"Red call"? I asked.

"Any call that exceeds the SLA time for handling is a red call, and gets reviewed with your manager at the end of the week. Manuel has a matrix with names down the vertical axis, and months across the horizontal. Each month we have to explain our over SLA minutes and what is being done to get them down. If anyone has too many minutes for too many months in a row, they are let go. We have to make our SLAs, or bonuses will not happen for workers and management, and our funding for the next year may be cut."

"What about the users and customers? Doesn't that hurt them"?

"You've got it backwards, Chris. You heard Jackie. She wanted action, not waiting. By having this SLA in place and managing to it, we are biased towards action in support of our users and customers. Users don't want to be on the phone, they want things done. That's our job, to get things done for the users, by getting them off the phone so they can drive the type of solution they desire. It's called empowerment."

It made sense in a strange way, but seemed different from what I had always thought was the right way to treat customers. But I knew how much I hated being kept on the phone by support, so Kourosh was probably right. And it actually made some sense when you thought about it in the context of what Lee had been trying to teach me.

"Well, what about your systems, you seemed to spend a lot of time shifting between them. Don't you have any integrated tools? Wouldn't that cut down on the time you take to serve your users"?

"We've added more functionality over time, but unfortunately these types of systems don't talk to each other very well; at least when you get beyond the sales hype."

"There are a lot of smart people in this company. Couldn't you have created some customization that links them into an integrated tool."

"That's a trap, Chris. If you customize beyond the vanilla, out of the box application, you quickly have a tool that can't be supported by the manufacturer, and in some cases, can't even be upgraded or patched without breaking something else. That's why it takes us a while to launch new initiatives or change processes. But we are committed and we always make it work. That's what the service desk does. We are the face of the company to customers and users." He leaned over to me. "And frankly, we do a right fine job of it, too. Just look at our SLAs. We publish them every day, week and month. There is no hiding for us. Everyone can see what a great job we are doing serving the customer."

"Well you clearly know how to make this all work. I never realized what a burden your teams had here. I'm impressed.

But what happens after you take the call? Suppose I call in and ask for a new employee computer set-up"?

Kourosh pointed to the large monitor at the other end of the room. "That 93% is the percentage of calls we resolve here."

"Why is it yellow"? I asked.

"We are on the verge of falling below our SLA. We'll just have to get more tickets closed at level one."

"But what about the ones you can't close, like complex alerts that need to go to senior technicians, or things you can't do here, like configuring PCs"?

"Between you and me, a closed ticket is a closed ticket, and that stops the clock. Sometimes we get too far down the road with a given ticket, and it's best if we discard it and start fresh. As Manuel says, it is less confusing for the user that way."

"So, you're saying to me that you game the system by closing out tickets that aren't being resolved, and making customers call back and start over with a new ticket"?

"No, absolutely not. It's not a new ticket. We know what happened before. It's merely refreshed, and because we are no longer under as much time pressure, we have a better chance of determining a resolution at our level. And that is good for the customer and the corporation."

"And for your goals."

"No one of us is as strong as all of us. We all succeed together much easier than separately."

"Okay, I get it," I said. "So if you can't resolve a ticket here, where does it go"?

"Those get escalated, and before you ask me to where, I'll tell you I don't know. We just tag the event and enter it into the system. From there it gets automatically routed to the right place. In the case of provisioning new employees, it's somewhere in Sue's team. She leads the desktop support team. But I can't tell you who it goes to, only that it goes into their queue. The automated system does the routing and assignment. Once it does that I can look it up and see the status, but we only have time to do that if someone complains. Besides, I know it goes to the right place; to the person best suited to resolve it. Of that I'm confident."

I gave Kourosh an incredulous look.

"Well, I'm pretty sure it goes to the right place, and if it doesn't, we hear about it, right"?

We both laughed.

"What about provisioning for new users? Where does that go"?

"Actually, most of the calls we get on that are from people who aren't smart enough to fill out the forms on the automated ordering site. IT did a really cool thing by setting up a configurator that admins can log into and pick exactly the set-up they need for their new employees. It's very complete and thorough, with hundreds of items in it. I saw one once and it barely fit in the binder, there were so many choices in it. How's that for service? And as long as they do it far enough in advance, and do it right, everything works out fine."

"Do the admins like it? Do you know if it makes their work easier"?

"They're supposed to get training on it as part of their job. Most of the calls we get from them are because they've goofed up the form, or don't know what they want, and ask us to decide," said Kourosh.

"Don't know what they want"?

"Yeah, like do they want solid state or mechanical drives, 6GB or 4GB of RAM, or even something as simple as how much processor power they need. We always try to direct them back to their boss for the answer, but sometimes even those managers don't know. Can you believe that? Here they are spending thousands of dollars of the company's money, and they have no idea what they want. Sometimes I wonder if they even know what they want their new employees to do. I mean, it is so simple even a child could do it."

"So what do you do if they are stuck"?

"It's up to the representative and the situation. I always max them out with the most powerful hardware and software available. That way they won't come back and complain their tools are too weak, and that's why they are missing their quotas."

I could see the logic in how Kourosh made his decisions. I was stunned that leaders in the company couldn't even plan for what kind of tools they wanted for their new employees. They'd better not let Lee find out.

I stood up and just before pulling my headset off, said, "Kourosh, I need to go. But thank you so much for sharing this with me, and helping me understand how hard the service desk works representing the company to the world."

"Glad to have helped," smiled Kourosh. "Please do me a favor, Chris. I have quite a few red tickets this month and the whole team is close to missing the SLA. If you could volunteer to Manuel what a great job we're doing, it might help during the monthly review."

I nodded and said, "No problem." Before I could finish shaking his hand, his screen lit up and he said, "Hello, you've reached the service desk. How may we help you today"?

Tips that would have helped Chris

Many ITSM systems you encounter will be legacy systems, or based on legacy systems, often hidden under a wrapper. That's where rather than re-write some functionality, a decision was made to simply write an interface which encloses the old application, in a face that makes it look new and modern to the user. Nothing changes under the hood.

Many times, the people responsible for the existing systems, or using the existing systems, will know little, if anything, about the system in question. Often the people who created the original core will be long gone, and there will be no supporting documentation.

People respond to the performance measures you set for them. So you must be very careful and thoughtful of what those measures are, and what behavior they will drive. Most SLAs, and other measures of process performance, tend to drive efficiency of the process (how fast it moves work through), rather than effectiveness (how well it provides benefits to the organization as a whole.). A process can be very efficient at pushing items through it, but the net result may have no value to anyone outside the process. This is because efficiency is much easier to measure than effectiveness, and most SLAs are either drawn up by process owners (who want to ensure the process is working well), or drawn up because they are easy to measure.

CHAPTER 10: DON'T PEEK BEHIND THE CURTAIN

"What do you want"? snapped Sue, without even looking up from her terminal. Her fingers never paused for a moment, as they jumped across the keyboard. Sue was manager of IT's desktop support team, and, judging by the cluster of people waiting outside her office, she was in high demand.

She followed up with, "You're blocking the door for people who need to see me. So move along and try to be productive, like maybe earning your pay, by doing whatever it is that you do."

I'd been unsuccessful setting up this meeting with her. She'd declined every invitation, and wouldn't take my calls. In desperation, I'd reached out to Lee, but even he wouldn't take my calls. Finally, I camped out at his office, and ambushed him when he arrived at work. That was enough for him to intercede with her leadership, and the meeting was arranged. His parting words to me had been, "You don't have what it takes to stand up to her. I won't be there, so I expect you will have a major fail, but that will be your fault, not mine."

I wondered if Lee had ever given anyone anything other than a putdown. Following Lee's advice was going to be hard, when he always ignored me and was dismissive of everything I did. He spent more time pandering to the executives than he did helping his team. And for me, that was the mark of a lousy manager. I knew he would get great personal joy from pushing me toward the exit, and I didn't even want to think about trying to find an interesting and decent, paying job in this market.

"I'm Chris. We have time scheduled, so I think I have priority over those people waiting to interrupt you, unless they have some kind of critical business issue. I'm here at the request of Jason and Jacob, to help sort out some concerns about equipment for the field that have become critical."

Sue stopped, turned her head, and scowled at me. "Critical? You don't know anything about critical. You ever have a corporate officer throw a fit worthy of the most truculent two-year old child, just because his mobile phone can't access the Internet for 30 minutes, between the time they clear security and the time they reach the boarding gate, so they end up missing two quarters of streaming basketball? You ever have a divisional VP try to get you fired because all of the division's laptops went down with viral attacks they picked up from her computer, after she let her daughter turn off the anti-virus on her laptop to download an illegal copy of a new movie as a Mother's Day present"?

She turned back to her screen and began typing again. "Come back and see me when you know something about priorities and critical issues. And get my manager's approval before you waste my time again."

I took a deep breath. I could call Lee and he would call her boss' boss, and force her to meet with me. But if I wanted anything more than simple "yes" and "no" answers, I needed her co-operation. If I made an enemy of her, I'd get nothing. If I folded, walked away, and tried to reschedule, I'd get nothing.

I sat down in the chair across the desk from her and said, "Sue, I want your attention for five minutes, please. And I am not leaving here until you give it to me."

She ignored me for a minute, but then looked up and asked, "You still here? Are you stupid or what"?

"I won't insult you and pretend you don't know why I am here, or who set this meeting up. If you help me, and give me a few moments of your time, I will do everything I can to reduce the number of complaints you get from the business about enabling new users. And given how this meeting was set up, I do have the ear of some people who can influence that. But I cannot help you unless you let me."

Sue stopped typing, and turned around in her chair. "Okay, there are 24 more minutes left in your time slot with me. Go for it."

"The issue is simple. People in the field are not getting the secure access, desktops, laptops, and tablets, on the days they requested, and people are complaining that the process is too hard and cumbersome." I pulled one of the documents from my folio. "I've got a note here from the central region VP, telling the CIO that he expects her to absorb the expenses of his new hire, who's spent the last week sitting around doing nothing because they weren't kitted up when they were supposed to be. The service desk ..."

"You can stop right there," she said. "The service desk may have a lot of desks, but it provides little service to anyone but themselves. All they do is complain and point fingers. Think about it. What value does the service desk possibly add for IT? Aren't we supposed to be in this together ... to have each other's back? They're supposed to be a buffer to keep us from idiot questions and constant interruptions, but they can't even do that."

"So what should they do with user questions and concerns"?

"Either know the technology, or trust those that do. Do you argue with your surgeon about whether to use interrupted, mattress or continuous stitches, when they sew you up after you've been in a car accident? No, of course not. You trust their training and knowledge in that particular area is greater than yours, and let them handle it. You tell them what you think is wrong, and then leave them alone until they tell you everything is fixed."

Sue took a deep drink from a dirty, stained coffee cup, that looked like it hadn't been washed in years. She reached into a cabinet and pulled out an enormous black vinyl, three-ring binder. The plastic cover was torn on one corner, and it was stuffed so full that some of the pages were starting to slide out. She slapped it down on her desk with a thud. It was the same binder Jacob had shown Lee.

"And so you won't think we're a bunch of anti-social geeks, take a look at this. It's the IT service catalog. It's got everything we do in IT. Anything that we could possibly do for users is in there, along with its costs, purpose, support levels and time to deliver. All those users need do, is select what they want on the appropriate request entry screen, and it gets taken care of. How hard is that? The service desk could do it. It's so simple, even a child could do it."

"Who has access to this"?

"All the admins got copies when we printed it up two years ago; service desk, too. So they all should be using it. If they're not, and they have problems, then it's their own fault. The users order some of the dumbest configurations you can imagine, and we don't have the time to do their work for them. And the service desk isn't smart enough to help them figure out what's right. That's why it can take so long. We have to make sense out of the nonsense they send us. You've gotta remember, our job is not to tell people what they need. Our job is to execute tasks. That's what our SLAs and goals are based on, and far be it from me to go against the wishes of leadership. If that's what they value, then that is what we execute."

Sue pulled a chart down that was taped to the wall beside her PC screen, and slid it across the table to me.

"Look at those KPIs. We are green all across the board this month, just like the last 18 months. We've never even come close to having a yellow. We have a fixed amount of time to accept, and then execute a legitimate request once it is assigned to the proper group. We meet that tight schedule almost without exception."

She leaned across the desk and smiled. "There's just one thing we can't fix here." She pointed a finger directly at me. "We can't fix ignorance."

I opened the binder. Kourosh had not shown me anything like this. Neither had Manuel. And I'd never seen an admin use one either. I'd seen Jacob give one to Lee, but this was the first time I actually got a look inside our service catalog.

Most of the pages were discolored, stained and worn. It seemed to be organized by the IT functional team; one section for network, one for storage, one for systems. Fortunately, there was a section for desktop and laptop systems. As a test to see if I understood what was in there, I tried to gather the information I'd need to order a laptop. I quickly jotted down a list of what I thought made sense and passed it to Sue.

"Would this be a good request and get me what I need for a new laptop"?

Sue scanned it and began shaking her head. "Not bad for a first try. But you can't use that much memory if you're only going to order a 32-bit operating system ... "

"So I can get something more than 32-bit"? I interrupted.

"Sure," said Sue, as she fanned deeper into the binder. "We've got 64-bit, too."

"And that would let me have more memory"?

"Obviously."

"But where do I find that"?

"Everyone knows that. But it doesn't matter because our VPN client doesn't support 64-bit anyway. So if you want the ability to connect with the rest of the world when you're not in the office, then you're better off sticking with 32-bit."

"So why are there three brands of laptops in here? I thought we didn't have a choice and were standardized on one."

"We don't. Actually there are four. What you see in there are two that we used to have when the catalog was first done. The third one was the one we were moving to, and now that's our standard, but we're retiring that one for another in three months, but it hasn't made it into the catalog yet."

"Huh? So two of the three available choices today are invalid, and the new option isn't even listed? You're making it easy for people to get it wrong."

"We need to show both the obsolete and the pending standards in our service catalog, so we can give Ian the information he needs to properly track assets. If you ask him, I'm sure he'd tell you that making sure none of the equipment disappears, is a lot more important than whether or not some sales rep can't watch videos on a laptop for a couple of days. We don't do anyone any favors by making it difficult for Ian, or the IT groups, to get the information they need to support the company."

"What about the changes to the catalog"?

"We haven't updated the catalog in a while. We've been too busy. Besides, we sent out an e-mail to everyone we sent catalogs to, so they should all know about it, or pass it on to those who do it now."

"And if they don't"?

Sue's voice got louder, and she started poking the catalog with her finger. "Then they should be ashamed of themselves. Each of us needs to do the best for the corporation. You just don't get it. This is a good deed that we did. None of our goals or objectives are tied to executing legitimate requests. If people aren't happy with the fact, they are too ignorant to know what they want. Then the source of the problem is with them and not us. It couldn't be plainer."

"But how can a user trying to kit-up a new employee, be expected to know all this? Do you see how they could get things confused"?

"Then they shouldn't have that job. You don't drive a car unless you know the rules of the road, and you shouldn't order equipment unless you know what you're doing. If they don't know, then find someone who does. And if they can't find someone, then get someone who does, or get some training. No one is born knowing any of this, and if I can learn it, then so can they."

Sue pulled down some creased and marked books on best practices. She grabbed the top one and waved it at me. "When we did the catalog, we specifically relied on best practice advice to communicate with the business in terms of services, so that's how we arranged the catalog. And unless I miss my guess, that is still best practice."

"So installing memory, or a hard drive, when building a server, is a service"?

"You got it. Just like us giving you a new laptop or desktop computer is a service." She jabbed a finger at one of the best practice manuals. "We are aligned with the other high-performing IT shops around the world. We are a textbook example of how to implement these best practices. I know. I've read them."

I had read the book Sue was poking with her finger. It was the latest guidance. I didn't remember all the specifics, but it would be unlikely she would claim to be in compliance with something I could so easily verify if she were not. I just couldn't let her know I didn't remember. It would be embarrassing and make me look weak if she thought I didn't know it by rote and had to look it up.

"Yep, you are right about that," I said.

Sue stuffed the best practice book back in her cabinet. "We're not going to waste any time trying to fix something that is not only done right, but is also aligned with best practice. Unlike you, we have real work to do."

Sue pulled the binder back from me and squeezed it into her cabinet before locking it, and the best practice book, inside. Looking up at the clock, she pointed to the cluster of people gathered outside her office. "Your time is up."

Tips that would have helped Chris

Miscommunication between people in IT and the business happens because they see the world through different contextual lenses. IT tends to see the world in terms of tasks and projects. However, their clients tend to see the world in terms of capabilities and activities. The former focuses on things with defined beginnings and ends, whereas the later views things as ongoing activities and deliverables. In other words, IT sees the business from an inside-out perspective, and the business sees IT from an outside-in perspective.

IT people tend to think of services in terms of products, platforms and projects they deliver, such that they view building a server as a service. Whereas from the business perspective, it's not a specific technology that is the service, it is the capability that technology provides. There should be several service catalog views, each relevant to their audience.

Make sure there is clarity on IT's role and responsibilities. Many times these fail because of failure to pull a RACI matrix together. A RACI matrix identifies which role is Responsible (Doer), Accountable (Owner), Consulted (Subject Matter Expert) and Informed (Gets Status Updates) for each activity and process. Be forewarned that some people don't like RACIs, because it prevents dodging ownership and accountability.

Documents, resources, catalogs and best practices, are not static objects. The moment you see them being locked up, unused, dusty, then you know there is no continual improvement and they are not being used as part of the ITSM process.

CHAPTER 11: KNOW WHAT YOU DON'T KNOW

It had been late afternoon when I left Sue's office, a couple of hours short of my normal quitting time. Rather than drive back to the office, I headed home. After all the extra hours I'd put in for this company, they owed me more time off.

They always kept harping about "work-life balance." Although, in practice, that too often seemed to mean after doing all this extra work, it's up to you to figure out how to balance all your other life obligations. But today, I was going to take them at their word. No one would know, and I needed time to think and decompress a little.

There was the added benefit of postponing what would be a very ugly conversation with Lee. I imagined his Cheshire Cat smile melting away, when I told him that new users in the field weren't getting set up when requested, because the business was too ignorant to ask for the equipment they needed. At least that was how the service desk viewed it. He'd have me out the door with his footprint marking my backside, before I had even finished the sentence, and have outsourced IT to some service provider before I reached my car, just for the fun of it.

It was raining hard and the roads were congested, so I was paying close attention to the cars around me, right up to the point where red warning lights turned my dash into a fiesta and most of my electronics shut down ... minor things like lights, wipers, and judging by the way the car handled, the power steering. I didn't want to think about what it had done to the power brakes.

The spray from the puddles and the rain was almost totally obscuring my vision. I decided to ignore the warning lights on the dash until traffic thinned out. Car repairs were expensive, but so were accidents. That decision lasted barely a minute, until acrid electrical smoke began drifting through the vents into the passenger compartment, reducing my vision even further.

Although I'd never been in a car fire before, I'd heard horror stories about them, and driven past a few of them on the highway. I turned on my directional signals. Thankfully, they worked. I struggled to turn the wheel enough to move towards the road's shoulder, but the driver beside me would not yield. In a moment of gallows humor, I wondered if he would yield once flames started coming out from under the hood … probably not. That's just the way people drive around here.

After what seemed like forever, I managed to force my way over to the shoulder. I killed the car engine, grabbed my phone and clambered out and over the guardrail. I recalled something about moving away, in case it really started to burn and exploded.

The rain was coming down in sheets now. I moved about a hundred yards down the shoulder away from the car, before I opened my cell phone and called for help. I stood there, soaked to the skin, as if I had been swimming with my clothes on. While I waited, I hoped my phone didn't burst into flames, too. Then I remembered I'd left my PC in the car, and, if it were lost, I'd probably have to pay the company back ... not to mention never being able to recover anything on it.

Fortunately, I escaped all that. The fire truck and the police arrived about the same time, and I spent the next 20 minutes standing in the rain, watching them soak down my car inside and out. It seemed surrealistically redundant, but they were the professionals.

Just before they left, the fire chief on the scene, an older man named Harold, assured me that in this case, although there was smoke, there was very little fire. It was an electrical meltdown, and I had probably inhaled a lifetime's worth of carcinogens in less than five minutes. Other than that, and what would probably be any enormous repair bill from a mechanic to replace the damaged wiring, plus the cost of the tow, there would be no lingering effects. I wasn't quite as confident in his judgment about auto mechanics as I was about his knowledge of fires.

15 minutes after the fire truck left, the tow truck from my dealership arrived, and towed me to the shop. But because I was dripping water like a leaky sponge, the driver wouldn't let me ride in the cab with him. I had to sit in the still-smoky stench of my car, complete with a broken passenger door window and soaked seat, courtesy of the fire department.

The tow driver unhooked my car at the shop. After consigning my car to their mechanics, and signing promises to pay for the work, I headed for the customer waiting area. Right now, all I needed was transportation and some good luck that the dealer was still open late during the week, and had the parts to get me back on the road tonight.

I pulled my car up, and was about to go look for one of the service reps to get things started, when I heard a very familiar voice speak in a very unfamiliar tone.

"Chris … is that you"?

I turned and could not believe what I saw. Coming down the hall from the garage area was Ramesh. That would have been strange enough, but he wasn't wearing his work clothes. He was wearing grey coveralls, spotted with grease and oil stains. It was not the image of the tyrant who had made my life miserable every day.

"Ramesh"? I asked tentatively.

"Yes, it's me," he said, wiping his hands with a greasy red rag, and then extending a hand, still smeared with layers of grime. The strangest part was that he was smiling, as if he were glad to see me. I'd never seen him smile before, even when he was hearing good news. It was creepy.

"What are you doing here ... " I paused for the right phrase, knowing what a proud man he was, and went with the most innocuous thing I could think of at the moment, " ... at this time of day"?

He leaned over and whispered, "Having fun." He chuckled and added, "But don't tell the people who own this place. They might figure there was something wrong with me and cut my pay."

"I don't understand. Are you telling me you work here now"?

"Yes", nodded Ramesh. "I worked as a mechanic years ago when I was in college. It was harder then. Today, you still have to do the physical work, but you also have to be able to master the digital tools and analysis. Some of these cars practically diagnose themselves for you."

"How come I've never seen you here before"? It was surreal talking to him now. Many people had been "set free to pursue further success in new environments," but once they were targeted for removal, no one ever spoke of them again, even after they left. It was as if they had some contagious disease, and even the use of their name would put you in the same condition. This was especially true for people in leadership positions.

"After Lee forced our CIO to fire me because he wanted me out of his way … "

I was stunned he used the word, "fired." Most people who'd been through that experience refused to talk about it as "fired," as if being fired automatically meant you had done something wrong; that simply being in the wrong place, at the wrong time, or in the way of someone else, could also get you booted out the door, and yet remain your fault.

"At first I was just hanging around the house feeling angry at Jessica for giving in to Lee, and feeling sorry for myself. I couldn't even bring myself to build a resume. Fortunately, my nephew, who is an accountant here at the dealership, told me how they were always looking for mechanics of any skill level. So I applied, and they signed me up. It's only been a couple of weeks, but to be honest, I wish I'd done this years ago."

"That's great," I said, trying to sound as earnest and heartfelt as possible. "I'm glad you're happy."

Ramesh leaned over and sniffed the air around me. "Phew. What a smell. You must have a wiring problem. I can still smell it on you. Catch fire or just a lot of smoke"?

I shared the adventure with him and was surprised to see him laugh. When I started to tell him of my relief that my laptop had not been destroyed, he interrupted me.

"Fudge them. I'm never going back there, and you should think about getting out yourself," he said. "The pay is less here, but I'm doing something that I never realized how much I loved. The expectations are clear, and as long as I get my work done according to the shop standards, my boss lets me alone. There's none of the back-stabbing, butt-kissing that the company seems to run on."

I was unsure what to say. This didn't seem like Ramesh at all. It was more like Ramesh had suffered a breakdown, and given up on everything he'd always believed in. They had really messed him up by letting him go like that. Initially I'd thought this was just part of the adjustment process, but the more he talked, the more I felt sorry for him. Not only had they kicked him out, but they had broken him, too. Sure he had made my life miserable, but I still didn't want to see him suffer.

"I'm really glad you've found something so fulfilling," was the best thing I could think of, and I crossed my fingers just hoping it sounded sincere enough.

"Honestly, I love it," he said, apparently not noticing my unease. "It is so much more fulfilling for me than what my old job had become."

"That's good to hear. I'm happy for you, Ramesh." I just hoped he could keep this job, so I wouldn't see him living on the street and pushing a shopping cart one day.

"Maybe you can help me," I said. "I'm really worried the car won't be ready tonight, but when I look at the line to talk to a service rep, it seems like it will be 30 minutes just to tell them what my problem is. If I can't get my car back, I am in deep trouble."

"Why don't you just use the self-service kiosk and get things started"? asked Ramesh.

Ramesh must have seen the look of confusion on my face, and walked me over to a kiosk with a terminal interface.

"I don't have to dumb this down, because you have a background in how databases and technology work. This kiosk gives you access to the database the dealership uses to manage the ongoing maintenance, recall and support for your car. It's just like the knowledge base they have at the service desk."

I thought about how well the service desk worked. My heart sank. I'd be here for weeks.

Ramesh punched in his access code, as well as my car's make, model, plate and VIN. A long and very detailed list of tasks that had been performed on my car at the dealership since the day I bought it appeared at the top, along with a detailed list of additional tasks at the bottom of the screen which were identified as needing to be done. Each task included the required parts, and standard time to complete the work. When Ramesh pressed a few other selections, a menu came up, asking what work needed to be done.

He grinned at me and said, "I'd guess wiring is the best place to start."

After selecting electrical, a long list of items appeared on the screen.

I scanned down the list of things; it was gibberish to me. "I don't mean to sound stupid, but these terms don't mean anything to me. I can barely make out the differences."

"Sorry," said Ramesh. "I was giving you the mechanic's view. It's obvious to me what these are," he said, as he rattled off the differences between the different service options. "It just defaulted to that because of my login ID. But you have no way of understanding what these mean. Let me log out and I'll log you in as a customer."

In a matter of moments, I was looking at a simpler set of choices.

"Go ahead," said Ramesh. "I'll bet you can figure it out without me saying anything to guide you."

There was less specific detail, but everything was bundled into groups that made sense to me. So I started by choosing "repair" over "maintenance," and then selecting, "electrical" over "body," "glass," and some other groups. I was surprised by one question. Rather than asking me what was wrong, it asked me what the symptoms were, and then the circumstances around the event that caused the need for "repair." It asked me if I were waiting for the car. And finally, if there were any other pieces of information I thought might help the mechanic.

When I pressed "OK," a copy of everything I had entered was shown on the screen, and I was given an opportunity to correct it. It was fine, so I simply pressed the button labeled, "submit." A few seconds later, a sheet of paper printed out of the machine, with a copy of my information, the date and time I'd submitted it, and the name and picture of the service representative who would be contacting me with updates. At the same time, my first name and repair number appeared on the monitors, scattered in strategic spots around the waiting area, showing when I entered the information, the status of my repair, and who was ahead of me.

"You got Maggie as your service rep. That's excellent," said Ramesh. "She's really good on the proactive follow-through. She'll keep you well-informed."

"I don't mean to offend, Ramesh, but this seems like an awful lot of work by the dealership just to make my life easier."

"Well, if you could get similar results, at similar costs, would you choose to use a dealership that made it easier for you, or easier for them"?

I laughed. "I've been to college. I can figure that out." I paused for a moment, and stared at the ceiling like I was thinking. "I'll take the one that makes my life easier."

"Even if the end result of the repair was the same"?

I nodded. "You have to ask"?

Ramesh smiled, "Course you would take the one that approaches this from your perspective, and not the dealer's. So would everyone. It's called "outside-in." That simply means everything you do is from the perspective of those who use your goods and services, not from the way that makes the provider's life easier. Most businesses discovered that a long time ago. But IT has a long history of working "inside-out," always using the perspective of what makes things easier for them. No business can survive treating their customers like that. IT got away with it for years, but not anymore. Those that don't make the switch, will end up getting outsourced to service providers that do put their users first."

I knew that Lee would think this was insane. No wonder he had gotten rid of Ramesh. If you let your users tell you what to do, you'll end up building a lot of out of date and incompatible customized things. It would be impossible to manage, and the cost of even trying would go through the roof. No business could survive that.

Maybe that was why Lee felt so strongly that you had to control your customers, and not the other way around. I guess there was some wisdom in what he had been saying. Maybe I had misjudged him after all.

Perhaps Lee had done the company a favor by getting rid of Ramesh. If he really believed this, then he sure didn't belong in a leadership position at the company. He'd take us all down.

Still, I didn't want to hurt him, so I just shrugged my shoulders. "I get it that users want things easier for them, but won't that create a lot of chaos? Won't everything become custom and impossible to manage"?

"Do you feel like we are dedicated to doing a great job for you"?

"Well, I feel like you're keeping me informed and part of the process, so I guess yes. I do."

"Doing it this way is not more work, it's just working in a way that's focused on the way the customer sees the world, and not on the way the mechanics do. The work is the same, and actually the customer has some skin in the game. They have to be part of the solution, but they don't mind because of the way they are treated. That lets the service reps do better quality work, and stop interrupting the mechanics so often, so we can get our job done."

Ramesh laughed, and it startled me. I couldn't remember hearing him laugh prior to tonight.

"Listen to me," he said. "I'm back to talking like a manager again. I'll have to work on fixing that."

"The thing I found interesting," I said. "Was that it never asked me what was wrong. How can you fix my problem if I don't tell you what's wrong"?

"That was my reaction the first time they showed it to me. But that lasted only until my first repair. That's when I realized I didn't want people to tell me the cause of their problem, because most of the time they didn't really know enough for it to be accurate, and it just sent me down the wrong path. I realized I'd rather just have them tell me what the symptoms were, and what was happening at the time ... the same questions I'd focus on if I were talking to them directly."

"Does that work"?

"So much simpler. If they want to share what they think the cause is, I'm happy to hear it. But most importantly, I need to know the symptoms and circumstances."

"Still, all this hardware and these applications, must have been expensive. The dealership must be making money by the bucket load to be able to afford it."

"Actually, it saves us money, because it makes us more efficient in our work, while at the same time, makes us more effective in meeting our customer's needs. It's a twofer – that's why it's imperative we do it. You can always find someone to fix your car more cheaply, and in the end the result is usually the same. For IT that means the results are similar, whether in-house IT does it, or a service provider does it. The only way IT will ever survive, is if they provide better service; provide you with a feeling that you are very important to them, and that IT is completely invested in their mutual success."

At that moment, a woman walked up to us. It was Maggie. I could identify her from the kiosk printout.

"Chris"? she asked.

"Just want to let you know the mechanic has finished diagnosing your car, and removing the bad wiring. There was a short where a piece of metal scraped off the wiring insulation over time. He's just beginning to put in the replacement. He's also going to replace your belts and hoses, just in case they were weakened by the excessive heat, and give everything else a quick check over to make sure you don't have a different problem the moment you leave here. It should be ready in about 90 minutes. Do you have any questions"?

As I shook my head, Ramesh said, "It's been great to see you Chris, but I've got to get back to work. I hope all goes well for you."

I watched Ramesh walk away from me and felt pity for him, and anger that they had broken him for no reason other than for Lee to demonstrate his power to the others in the organization. But after listening to him babble all that inside-outside-backwards-forwards nonsense, I knew they had no choice. I just wish they had put him in an easier role at the company, rather than giving him the boot.

I filed that information away for my own benefit. Any weakness, no matter how small, would not be met with compassion and consideration. If I showed the slightest fault, they would boot me out.

11: Know What you Don't Know

It was going to be survival of the fittest and it looked like I needed to pick a side.

Tips that would have helped Chris

One way to view the difference between IT having an inside-out vs. and outside-in approach, is to think about inside-out as being focused on making IT as efficient as possible in serving the business. Outside-in, on the other hand, is focused on making IT as effective as possible in supporting the business. You can spot this in an instant, by looking at the KPIs, dashboards and scorecards IT uses to measure its performance. If most of them measure how efficient the IT processes run, then you are probably an inside-out organization. You need some efficiency measures, but they should be offset by a strong overweighting of measures of the effectiveness in IT driving business goals. The old idea that if IT does its job well, it is supporting the business, is no longer enough in the 21st Century.

Beware those who profess to follow outside-in, but in practice, do not. This includes both internal IT departments, as well as outside service providers. Due diligence, and thorough inspection of the reality behind the claims, is essential.

Whether by incident or request, keep the clients from performing root cause, or designing the solution. That is your job, not theirs. Understand their desired outcome. Like a doctor, you must focus on the situation, and the symptoms presented, so you can determine how best to handle the client's need.

CHAPTER 12: A FOOL WITH A TOOL IS STILL A FOOL

After keeping me waiting for 20 minutes, Lee's admin opened the door to his office, and Lee wordlessly gestured me on in.

It had been a beautiful day outside, and now the sun was going down. The light flowing in was a blend of orange and gold, that lit up every object it touched, making them glow as if from within. Lee's office was arranged so that in the afternoon, when the light came directly in through the huge windows, it came in over his shoulders. This did two things. If you were meeting with Lee, the glare from the light made you squint, and it made him glow as if the light were radiating from him.

It wasn't until I looked away, out of the direct light, that I saw Crayton sitting over by the window. He had been in here talking with Lee all of the time I had been kept waiting outside. I wondered what they had been talking about. I hadn't seen much of Crayton since Lee had taken my Rubber Boots project away and given it to him. I tried to assume good intentions, but I was still concerned, especially since Crayton was the one person I had talked to about the proposal I was planning for Lee. I'd asked Crayton for help in finding weak spots, and now, the day I go to pitch it to Lee, Crayton is in there chatting up Lee beforehand.

I caught myself. I was assuming bad intent. Crayton was not the kind of person to rock the boat. He was just hanging on for a couple of years till retirement. There was no reason for him to steal my idea, or plot against me ... was there?

Lee gestured for me to sit across the desk from him. Surprisingly, he waited patiently for me to get settled, then asked, "So I understand you wish to propose a solution; a solution that will give the field control over what they get and when. Am I correct"?

I nodded.

I struggled to keep a calm exterior. Crayton had spilled everything to Lee. I wondered what he'd gotten in return from Lee, because that is the way Lee worked. I'd only reached out to two people for feedback before speaking to Lee. They were Sean and Crayton. And with Crayton right here talking to Lee just before I walked in, the source of the leak was obvious.

By watching Lee, I'd learned that unique information others don't hold was the basis for power and influence in the company. And if there was one thing more important to Lee than money, or company success, it was power and influence.

"And I trust you were happy to see Ramesh again, or do you still hold grudges"? asked Lee.

He'd caught me completely off-guard. "How did you know"?

"We talk on a regular basis."

I was stunned. Ramesh had not mentioned they had an ongoing dialogue. Did it mean that Ramesh was sending him regular reports? How else could Lee have known so fast? Or was my boss lying to me?

"But you fired him," I managed to say.

"Good to hear you speaking plain and not through euphemisms. Try to remember that the single most helpful and important person to you when you take over anything, whether it is a project or organization or a process, is the person you replaced."

Lee turned to Crayton and said, "We've already covered most of this. Why don't you get that task we just talked about taken care of, in anticipation of our visitors this afternoon"?

Crayton packed up his material and headed for the door. "Got it," he said. "See you this afternoon."

After Crayton closed the door behind him, Lee asked, "Always build a relationship with the person you replace, even if you fired them. Who do you think knows more about where the bodies are buried, where the alliances are, who the weak links are; all the things you need to know but can only be learned through experience. Your opportunities for success are increased dramatically if you have that human cheat sheet. You don't have to repeat everyone's mistakes to learn from them."

"Doesn't he hate you for what you did to him"?

"That's a leadership art; separating someone from the company without making an enemy of them. It's all in how well you convince them that this isn't really your idea; that you fought for their retention, but that others are behind it. Sometimes you can even convince them their own staff forced it to happen, by complaining to senior leadership – even better if you can convince them their staff disliked them so much, the tales they told senior leadership about you were lies. And then of course, like any good game of "Slap 'n Tickle," you do some small things for them when they leave, offer to be a reference, or contact some of your friends on their behalf. You'd be amazed at how much people will give up and trust you for the tiniest little favors. It's all selling. Everything we do, every day in every way, is selling our needs and wishes to others. If you can't sell that, then you don't belong in a leadership role here, or anywhere else. You're just meant to be another sheep, not a shepherd."

I was confused. I couldn't tell if Lee was right, really evil, or if it even mattered. But I was here, and had to deal with Lee in a way he would value, or my solution would never see the light of day.

Perhaps seeing the quizzical look on my face, Lee added, "Did Ramesh seem unhappy in his new role"?

"He claimed he wasn't, but I know he was lying."

"Really"? asked Lee, his grin seeming to grow. "And why was that"?

I saw the trap as soon as Lee said it. He was trying to get me to say something bad about him for letting Ramesh go and breaking him in the process. I was not going to fall into it.

"He just seemed resigned to his job. I don't know his personal circumstances. Perhaps he needed the money. It was just a feeling that he didn't belong there; that there was a better, higher use for his talents."

"Is that so"? asked Lee, nervously tapping a pencil against the surface of his desk. "Did he tell you that the owner of the dealership is a close personal friend of mine; that he knew that, and asked me to personally intervene to help get him that position? Which I did, of course."

Stories weren't matching. But why would Lee lie? Why wouldn't he lie? He was capable of it. Of that, I was sure.

12: A Fool With a Tool is Still a Fool

But such a specific, easily checkable falsehood went against everything I knew about him. And why would Ramesh lie? He had nothing to gain. But I wasn't going to let Lee see my confusion. He couldn't see my weakness.

"Thanks for the advice," I said, and switched subjects. "We need to get this solution out in front of the field, so they can understand what we're doing, and give us the okay to get it in place."

"Don't worry," said Lee. "I have that under control."

"Okay. Are you planning on having me go through this with the field soon"?

"Nothing immediate. Let's set up a time this afternoon when you can come by and run through your proposal, as if you were presenting it to field representatives. There are some others I would like to be part of this. Then we can give you some constructive feedback."

We set the meeting for 3.00 pm that afternoon.

As I walked out of his office, I turned and asked Lee, "When I came in, I noticed you had Crayton working on something. Should I ask him to put that on hold for the afternoon and participate in this? He has been useful as a sounding board."

Without looking up from his desk, Lee said, "If I were you, I would spend less time worrying about Crayton's situation, and more time worrying about your own. I'll ensure that Crayton's priorities are appropriate for him."

Walking back to my cube, I couldn't help but think that all things considered, it could have gone a lot worse.

It was only 2.40 pm as I hurried down the hall toward Lee's office. I was going to be early, but that often happened when I was nervous. And there was good reason to be` nervous. I was ready to present my proposal for a service catalog tool for the field; a tool that offered things using the lexicon of the field, rather than that of IT; a tool that would ensure IT got exactly what it needed from the field. Because only by giving each group a view of services that made sense to them, via a tool that translated from one view to another, would it work. It made perfect sense. If you understood what you were seeing, you could make better decisions.

Most importantly, blaming the current tools for the problem minimized the finger pointing at any one person. People cared if you called them out as the source of an issue. It made them look bad in front of their peers and their leaders. Tools had no feelings or egos to get hurt, and in this case, where the creator of the old tool was long gone, there should be no one to take offense. It was the perfect solution.

When I got to Lee's office, the door was open, but he was not inside. His admin glanced at me and then focused back on her computer, before saying, "What are you doing here? Your meeting was cancelled."

"What"?

"I just sent you a note from Lee, canceling your meeting. He had some people come in from the field, and he's meeting with them instead." She fumbled with her keyboard, but didn't take her eyes from the screen. "It was something about catalogs. You'll see it when you get back to your cube and check your mail."

"Where are they meeting"?

"It's in the e-mail," she huffed, as if annoyed that I was asking her to do something. She looked through her mail files for a moment, then said, "Wait, here it is. They are meeting in the corporate sales and marketing conference room."

That was bad. The problem was, it was not open to the masses. Only select admins had access to the schedule, and to get to the door you had to run a gauntlet of them, and from what I'd heard, believed their mission in the world was to protect and restrict access to that sanctuary, with their lives if necessary.

"Who's there"?

"It's just Lee and two of the regional field VPs ... oh, and Crayton is with them, too. I think they are talking about catalogs, or lists, or something like that. I just know that Lee was very excited after talking with Crayton this morning."

Crayton. So my fears had been justified. He was one of the few people I had talked to about my idea. It looked like he was taking my idea and grabbing credit for it.

I was not going to let him steal my idea.

Without even thinking about how to do that, I headed to the Board Room. It was a stupid thing to do. I knew it was a stupid thing to do, but I could not let go of the idea of Crayton stealing my idea, and getting credit for it. Of course, I didn't really create it. A car dealer did, and it was Ramesh of all people that showed it to me, and explained how it worked. But that was beside the point.

I quick-walked down the hall, hoping that perhaps I could catch them before they started, or maybe during a break. I was sure that, if I could get Lee alone, I could make him understand that this was my idea, not Crayton's, and the credit should go to me. Surely, he would understand and set things right.

I was nearly out of breath by the time I got near the room. I stopped, took a moment to center myself, then casually turned the corner and walked down the corridor. The hallway dead-ended at the Board Room's door. Directly in front of it sat a woman behind an impeccably neat desk. She was sitting with her hands carefully folded on her desk in front of her, as she stared almost unblinkingly straight ahead. She could have been a mannequin for all I knew.

I walked up to her, wearing my most confident face; as if I was in the room every day and I was expected inside immediately.

She looked up from the sheet of paper on her desk and pushed her glasses back up her nose. With a tone and a look that would stop a rolling boulder, "May I help you"? In my mind, I imagined her tensing, ready to throw herself in front of the door and pummel me into submission using some ancient, fighting technique if I got too close.

"I'm late again. Have they started the meeting without me"? I was proud of that line. It was pure Lee. No lies to get trapped in, no falsehoods to be called on; just a snippet of incomplete information to which she would hopefully fill in the blanks and presume I merited entry.

But she was well trained and experienced. "And which meeting is that"?

"Lee is chatting with some folks from the field." I peered around her and noticed the room was empty and dark.

"And you are"?

12: A Fool With a Tool is Still a Fool

"My name is Chris. I work for Lee and he asked me to deliver a presentation."

She scowled, and after consulting the schedule on her computer said, "Well, the room is not available at all today. It is fully booked. Perhaps you should try one of the other conference rooms." She turned back to the papers on her desk, and without looking up, or waiting for a response, said, "Sorry I could not be of more assistance. Have a nice day."

I stood silent for a moment, not quite sure what to do. I turned and slowly walked back down the corridor, playing out options in my head. I was almost out of ideas. I sent Lee a text, but nothing came back, so he was either in a meeting or ignoring me. I even sent one to Crayton, but he was silent, too.

I didn't know what to do. There had to be some way I could prevent them from stealing my idea. I had come too far for it to end this way. I started walking back down the hall.

I was so caught in my own thoughts that I nearly walked past them. There, in the break room, sitting around a table, were Lee, two suits wearing visitor badges, and Crayton. And in the middle of it all was Sean, who seemed to be doing most of the talking and gesturing. At least he had the full attention of Lee and the suits. That meant they probably weren't talking about the role relevant service catalog idea of mine.

I hesitated for a moment, unsure if I should break into their meeting. It was a huge breach of corporate etiquette, especially if they were talking about something else. I was going to walk away, but then I could hear Lee's voice in my mind.

"The trick to survival in the modern corporation is not to live by the rules. The trick is to not get punished for breaking them. If they don't catch you, or you were very successful, then you have nothing to worry about."

I walked into the break room and acted as if I had just stumbled upon them. I heard Crayton talking about a service catalog with role-relevant views. I couldn't believe what he was doing. I had actually thought he was an ally.

I pulled up a chair, and sat down in the middle of the group. Before Lee's face of surprise and irritation could change into words, I reached out to the two suits and introduced myself. "Hi, my name is Chris. I'm part of Lee's team."

The man in the blue suit introduced himself as Henrik and the one in the grey suit introduced himself as Obasi. Their clothes had the mild style variations one saw from country to country, and were definitely not from around here.

I gave everyone my best smile and said, "I hope I'm not interrupting, but I accidentally overheard Crayton speaking about service catalogs. I've done a lot of work on them and have some ideas you might be interested in."

Henrik shrugged his shoulders. With a pronounced Saxony accent, he said, "I am very pleased to meet you, Chris. However, you should know I am not really interested in a service catalog, or any other tool IT uses. I only wish for my teams to have the support from IT that they request, when they request it. How IT provides that is of no interest to me. I measure IT as I do my own organization, by results."

"I couldn't agree with you more," I said. "That's why I have a proposal to use a different type of service catalog. Not that bloated obsolete notebook your teams may have suffered through in the past. I'm talking about something new, where the only thing your teams will see, are the services relevant to them, and expressed in terms they will resonate with. They won't have to figure out a long list of IT technical items. And by getting the order the way IT expects it, our SLAs for delivery will finally be meaningful. That means better quality, better results, and faster delivery."

I glanced at Crayton. I wondered how much he liked me stealing my idea back.

"It sounds like Sean and Crayton have already briefed you. That is excellent," said Obasi. Turning to Lee he said, "Congratulations on fitting in so soon. With such a high degree of communication and alignment across different groups in the IT organization, you're clearly succeeding. Just make sure it is mobile-friendly, so it fits with our roll-out of tablets to the entire sales force in my country over the next six months."

Lee puffed himself up a little, and put his hand on my shoulder. To a casual observer it could have been a gesture of support. But the way he pressed down and his fingers dug in, it was clearly a gesture of dominance. "It wasn't me. I can't take any of the credit," said Lee. "None of this would have happened without such a great team under me."

Crayton followed Lee's lead. "It was Sean's insight and experience that drove this. He brought the reality of IT capabilities to it. I'm just the concept person here who followed Sean's lead."

Henrik interrupted, "You are getting ahead of yourself. Budgets are very tight this year. Right now, I get an allocated charge that bears no resemblance to which IT products I use and how often. I must have control over the cost. I must have ways to reduce the IT cost. I am not asking you to reduce your charges. I am simply asking that increases or decreases in my utilization of IT products, be reflected in my charges. Let me control my own destiny."

"That sounds very reasonable," offered Lee. "And if IT were being paid for specific items, they would be much more accountable to deliver them consistent with the SLA."

"That is correct," said Obasi. "Today I pay a fixed allocation and do not have to worry about IT overcharging me, and preventing me from meeting my business objectives because their costs are bloated. If I must pay by item, then I want to see IT have the same price efficiencies we are forced to work with in the field. Anything else is not fair."

Sean shook his head. "You are getting a bargain now. IT insulates you from worrying about our charges. As long as you budget what we tell you to, you can plan accordingly and be secure for the entire year."

"With all respect, you do not understand what it is like in the field," said Henrik. "We must respond to competition, customer sentiments, business conditions, and a host of other dynamic variables. We must be flexible enough to change day to day. The company cannot tolerate us moving so slowly that we only change once a year. We cannot slow our customers down; we need to match their speed. IT must do the same."

Sean picked up the worn binder, containing the old service catalog, from Crayton's pile of materials. "Look at this. The cost to track the cost, and price each one of these items, means we'll have to add more overheads, and we'll have to cover the overheads in our charges to you."

Obasi said, "I would consider that a reasonable trade-off for control over which of those items we truly want."

"Even if you don't realize, you may need some items whether you like it or not," said Sean.

Then it hit me ... Dim sum and the auto repair.

"That doesn't have to be a problem," I said, snatching the binder from Sean. "IT may need to understand all these bits, but that doesn't mean the field must also. What if IT built a collection of business results – driving solutions, instead of a gigantic list of tools used to create the solutions"?

I opened the binder and fanned through the pages. "I'm talking about things like collaboration, training, hosting and such; even kitting up users with the right technology. We could have maybe 10 or 20 of these. And each of them would have a pre-packaged set of alternatives, arranged in tiers. That way the business could pick from a smaller list of alternatives, from categories that represent the issue needing to be solved, rather than gigantic lists of tools to solve issues."

Heads started nodding, and I soon lost track of time as we sketched out a rough idea of how it might work; the language that made sense to the field, the bundles that IT would need to work with, and even some cuts at rough pricing. People came and went through the break room, but they were just a blur. And every time I caught a glimpse of Lee, he seemed to be scowling at me. Clearly, I'd disrupted the plan he'd put in place. It felt good.

12: A Fool With a Tool is Still a Fool

Obasi looked at his watch, stood up and turned to Lee. "We have been at this for several hours now, and we have accomplished much today. Thanks to you, Lee, for pulling this all together for us. I have one more item we need."

"Anything for you, Obasi," said Lee.

"We need this to get into the project pipeline immediately. This cannot be another one of those items that disappear into the home office bureaucracy. Surely you understand the importance of action."

Lee smiled at me and said, "Not a problem. Although this is really a change in service process, it needs to go before our Project and Service Initiation Review Board. I'll have Chris make sure an appropriate proposal is prepared, and made part of the PSIRB agenda at their next meeting."

Lee turned to me, checked his watch, and smiled. "And that meeting is tomorrow morning. I'm sure that for an expert such as Chris that should not be a problem. I promise you that Chris will get an approval for the initiative to immediately move into prioritization. I'm sure Chris knows the right levers to pull."

Obasi nodded. "Excellent. Once again, Lee, you have exceeded our expectations."

I checked the time. It was the end of the day. Lee had just committed me to an impossible task, in front of some senior leaders. If I failed, it was my fault. If I somehow managed to pull it off, he looked like a hero for giving it to me. I was being set up to fail and he couldn't lose.

Tips that would have helped Chris.

Communications should always be in role-based language. It is not up to the business to learn how IT works internally. Just as the business does for the company's customers, it is up to IT to package what it does into units, relevant to the business' need, and present it in terms that describe how it provides benefits, that directly drive towards the business' goals.

Provide the business with choices in groups that represent real alternatives. If providing websites on request to the business, an appropriate question is whether they want it quickly, with limited interactivity, or later, with full e-commerce and interactive functionality, or fully customized. Don't provide the business with a layer of choices for providing websites, such as whether they want robust e-commerce, or high availability, or role-relevant views. Each of those choices is really part of its own layer of alternatives.

One way to view the difference between IT having an inside-out vs. outside-in approach, is to think about inside-out as being focused on making IT as efficient as possible in serving the business. Outside-in, on the other hand, is focused on making IT as effective as possible in supporting the business. Look at the KPIs, dashboards and scorecards IT uses to measure its performance. If they measure how efficient the IT processes run, then you are probably an inside-out organization. You need efficiency measures, but they should be offset by strong measures of the effectiveness in IT driving business goals. The old idea that if IT does its job well it is supporting the business, is no longer enough in the 21st Century.

CHAPTER 13: BOILING THE OCEAN, A SPOONFUL AT A TIME

I was robbed of credit for all the good work I did, and then set up to fail on an impossible task that I had nothing to do with.

There was no way I could put a workable proposal together by the morning, and, even then, get that committee to sign off on it. They had a reputation for saying no to just about everything.

It didn't seem to have much to do with the merits of the proposals, and probably had more to do with being their way of keeping the workload in IT manageable.

As I headed back to my cube, I wasn't sure which was worse. But right now it looked like tomorrow would be my last day employed at the company.

As I walked slowly back to my cube, that was the only thought in my mind. That Obasi and Henrik liked the idea made no difference. No one would believe it was my idea now. No one was going to give me credit for all of the hard work I'd put in. All of those endless conversations and interviews didn't mean anything. And then, when my presentation failed, my defeat would be complete.

Sean and Crayton, the two people I had trusted with my ideas, were going to get credit for the idea of using a role relevant catalog to improve the field experience. And of course, by reflection, Lee would get a substantial share of the credit, too. All I would get would be some minor notes, as the grunt who assembled the parts based on their direction and then couldn't deliver in the end.

Lee had abandoned me. All he'd needed to do, was to say something to Obasi about how he had chosen me to resolve this, and, despite long odds, I had made it work ... that I was the champion of the hour.

Instead, the best I'd gotten were some comments by Henrik about how lucky I was to be able to see how these people worked and learn from them.

I was almost back to my cube when Sean walked up and stopped in front of me.

"Hey, I wanted to know if you needed any help in getting that presentation ready for tomorrow morning."

I resisted the urge to hit him, but I wasn't going to just take it and walk away silently. "That's pretty generous for someone who just stole credit for my work. What do you have in mind; stealing the credit for Review Board approval if that is successful, too"?

"Those are pretty harsh words from someone whose butt I just pulled out of the fire," said Sean.

I just shook my head. "I'm not that stupid."

"Seriously. When Crayton told me you were meeting one-on-one with Lee to review your proposal for the role relevant view service catalog, I knew you were about to get shafted."

"Keep going," I said. "I want to see how you are going to dig yourself out of this hole."

"Because central to your idea, as you explained it to me, is the concept of business-facing services. Well, not only does Lee have no clue as to what a service is, or is not, the members of the PSIRB are equally as ignorant, and consider the whole concept a lot of bureaucratic and academic nonsense, that has no relevance to the way we do business. Something along the lines of, we've never needed this distinction in the past, so why should we waste resources on doing something that has no relevance in the real world"?

"So what," I said. "You don't even know the definition of a service."

"You think so"? asked Sean. "Are you talking about user-facing services, or internal IT-facing services"?

"User-facing. That's what we're concerned about here."

"Practical or academic"?

"Put it in a way the Review Board would understand," I said.

"I'll do it in a single sentence. A bundle of activities based on IT capabilities, and expressed in user-relevant terms that directly help them achieve their goals. They are defined outside-in."

"That'll do for now, but we'll need to talk some more."

"Don't be an arrogant jerk," said Sean. "How do you think I know about how the Review Board views the concept of client-facing services?"

That was a bit I would need to think about. "Okay, but what about Lee? Client-facing services are what Lee keeps harping to me about."

"Lee was setting you up to fail in public. He doesn't really care about services. All he cares about is Lee getting ahead."

"And why would he want to do that? He can fire me anytime he wants."

"True, but Lee only fires people when it suits his purpose, and then he makes sure it's done in a public, or at least noticeable, way. Firing you after the field leaders see a weak representation of the business' needs, makes him seem that much more effective in their eyes. He's working on improving his image with the only people who matter in his eyes, and you just happen to be convenient. Nothing personal, as he would say."

"That's a pretty weak story. And how did you come to this conclusion – telepathy? You've spent less time with Lee than I have, and Ramesh spent more time with me in a week than Lee has in two months."

Sean folded his arms and smiled. "Because I spoke to the people in the field that worked for him before he came here. They're old friends of mine."

In the perverse calculus of Lee's view of the world, it all seemed to make sense. Leaving bodies in your wake, especially if they were home office, non-revenue producing bodies, was a way to demonstrate to the field how much influence you had over the company, and how focused you were on giving the field operations exactly what they needed. It was plausible, but was it true?

"What about Crayton"? I asked. "He was acting like I'd never existed. In fact ... ," I pointed a finger at Sean. "He gave you the credit for all the ideas and proposals."

"Poor Crayton. All Crayton wants is to hang on for a couple more years, so he can get his pension and his retirement medical. Lee knew that from the start, so whenever he wants more information, he squeezes Crayton with threats of firing. It works. Crayton does whatever Lee wants. How do you think Lee knew to cancel your meeting? You were still going to get stuck with this assignment, he just didn't want you to meet anyone, or talk to him about it, beforehand. But then you showed up in the break room and he had to improvise."

"Sorry, Sean. Your story doesn't fit. Crayton kept promoting you as the creator of the ideas, not me. And I was right there."

Sean stood silent for a moment, and then said, "That's true. I was as surprised as anyone. Lee was probably apoplectic inside, but he's good enough not to show it." Sean stared at the ceiling for a moment. "I don't have any answer for you. I guess you'll have to ask Crayton." Sean paused, grinned, and added, "Of course you could always ask Lee if his master plan had been thwarted."

"Very funny. Besides, Lee won't talk to me unless he wants something."

The bigger question was whether or not I could trust Sean. His story was weak and full of holes. But there were parts of it that seemed so right.

"So," said Sean. "Do you want some help or not? Cause if you don't, there is a pint of beer waiting for me on the way home, and it's looking better and better by the minute. So you better make up your mind."

Sean and I spent the next six hours pulling together a proposal for an initiative the Review Board could approve and establish as a project ready for prioritization. Much as I hated to admit it, he was good, and we worked well as a team. It was really coming together and was objectively much stronger than I would have been able to prepare myself. He'd even used his personal friendship with the meeting scheduler to get it on the agenda, despite it being past the cut-off date for being considered at tomorrow's meeting. That was something I could not have achieved. So he seemed to be earnest in his desire to help.

But every hour or so, he'd get a text message and then wander off to make a call. I couldn't tell if it was suspicious; that he was really in league with Lee, who was checking up on us, or if he just got a lot of calls. The whole experience with Lee, with all the plots and sub-plots, felt like it was poisoning my ability to work with other people in an open and honest way. In his world, you didn't collaborate, you manipulated, and I didn't like that at all.

It was late when we finished the proposal. I thought it was pretty good. Sean rated it barely mediocre, but we were both too tired at that point to argue over it.

"Let's go through it in the morning," I suggested.

"The pig won't get any prettier," said Sean. "But it is probably as good as we can do for now."

I was too tired to snap back at him and left it at, "I'm going home. You can keep working if you want."

Sean checked the time and said, "Nope, that pint is still waiting for me. If I hurry and get there before they close, it won't go to waste."

I grabbed some papers and headed toward the door. As I passed him, Sean said, "The proposal may be miserable, but it's not all your fault. You worked hard on it. I've got to give you credit for that."

I just nodded and headed into the parking lot.

I put started my car and headed for the parking lot exit. I dialed Crayton's number before I made it to the street. I didn't care how late it was, I needed to check Sean's story against his.

"Hello," mumbled Crayton, in a sleep-fogged voice.

I was wired on too many energy drinks and it showed.

"What the deal, Crayton? Why'd you do it"?

"Huh"?

"Today, at the meeting with Lee and Sean and those two suits. Why didn't you give me credit for all my work? I trust you by asking for your feedback. I deal with you transparently, and you cut me off at the knees. Why did you do it"?

I hadn't realized how angry I was about what had happened.

"I don't understand," said Crayton. "Aren't you doing a presentation about that tomorrow"? There was a moment's hesitation, I mean today."

I checked my watch. It was almost 1.30 am. No wonder Crayton had been in bed.

"Look, Chris. I just did what Sean asked me to do. He told me that someone needed to talk about the idea, and that I was the perfect person to do it. You weren't there, and I guess he didn't want Lee's group to look disorganized or something. I don't know."

"You mean he asked you to give him credit for leading the effort"?

"No, I did that. I thought it made the whole things seem much more organized. I just figured that would make Lee look good; like he had a focused task-force responding to the needs of the field. You know how much he talks about that."

"Why would you do that? Why do you care"?

I couldn't believe what I was hearing. If it were true, why hadn't Sean mentioned it? Someone was lying to me, either intentionally or through ignorance.

"Chris, you don't know what it is like. You've got a lot of work years left in you. If they fire you tomorrow, you can always get a job someplace else. Me, I'm less than two years from retirement, in an industry where businesses won't hire people my age. I have to start over. Most likely I'll be forced into early retirement and live the rest of my life broke."

Crayton paused for a moment. I thought I could hear some quiet crying on the other end of the phone.

"I can't do that to my wife, and my kids, and grandchildren. Please show some compassion. Please don't be like Lee."

I wasn't sure what Crayton was talking about. Did he really believe I had the ability to have him fired? Perhaps he was afraid I was in league with Lee.

I was torn by a weird melange of pity, sympathy and disgust. Crayton was a broken man, and the irony was he still had his job. Unlike Ramesh, who seemed to savor his freedom, the thought terrified Crayton. And Lee didn't have to do a thing to make him that way.

"Go back to sleep," I said. "Don't worry. You did fine today. We'll talk tomorrow ... make that later today." I'd lied, but there was no truth I could tell him that would not make matters worse. As I pulled into the parking lot for my apartment, I wondered if that was what Lee had intended for Ramesh, and was trying to create for me? And what was Sean's agenda? But most of all, I just kept wanting to know why we didn't take all this time we wasted on drama, and spend it making the company better. It made no sense.

Tips that would have helped Chris

It's important to be observant. You can learn much simply by watching how others around you respond to different situations. This lets you benefit from their experience, without having to go through the exact same event. Just be careful that you reach the right conclusions. Your observations are facts, and you may, or may not, have all the facts you need to reach the right conclusion. It is easy to jump to a conclusion that teaches you the wrong lesson from their experience. That is the risk of learning from the actions of others.

Don't assume there is a conspiracy around every corner, and that every action is a Machiavellian attempt to take advantage of you.

Sometimes leaders appear to be playing favorites. Sometimes it is real. And sometimes it is done to convey a message to others inside, or outside the group. And sometimes it's just a perception.

CHAPTER 14: CHANGE IS HARD

Sean met me outside my cube, and we walked together to the room where the PSIRB was meeting. It was over in the executive part of the building, a place I'd never been to before. I'd tried to call Crayton, but he was not responding.

"You've got a really tough audience in there," said Sean. "They won't give you a second chance if you slip up anywhere."

I stopped and grabbed him by the arm. "What do you mean me? My recollection is that we both worked on this into the late hours last night, or was I hallucinating from too much energy drink"?

"Now I'm confused," said Sean with a grin. "I thought you were the one last night who was accusing me of stealing your ideas and taking credit for them ... as I was helping you even though you hadn't asked. And now you want me to have part of the credit"?

I was wedged. Nothing fit exactly together. No matter what I did, the facts wouldn't align. And to make matters worse, I had instinctively, without considering the ramifications, asked Sean to help me with the presentation. This was all Lee's influence. I was seeing plots and assassins in every corner. I was really beginning to wish I'd never met him.

Sean followed up before I could respond. "Look, I'm just playing with you. I know from others who've gone in there that the Review Board likes to keep the meeting small. That way they can have an open and frank discussion."

Sean leaned over and whispered, "That means they curse at each other and yell, and generally act in ways they don't want the vast majority of people to see, for fear of looking imperfect. For some reason they live under the delusion that the average worker thinks they are flawless, and only speak in measured leader-like tones. Personally, I think they spend too much time with themselves. You've gotta remember, the PSIRB has only been in place since about six months before Lee arrived. They're still learning to work together. Their sole purpose is to give the executive leadership cover when the field gets upset."

"Try not to make me feel too optimistic. After all, last night you thought the presentation sucked."

"It's fine," said Sean. "I just know that you could propose turning lead into gold at no cost to the company, but unless some field manager had requested it, they'd tell you, not this year. You gotta remember, they aren't there to add more things to the queue of work; their job is to keep things off the table. Any excuse will do. The only thing they might not deny this year is field requests."

"If you know people who went through this before, what kind of success rate did they have"? I asked.

Sean shook his head, "Only those that originated in the field, even got considered. Nobody got approval. Everyone got told to try again next year."

"So maybe I've got a chance. This is a direct response to Lee's objectives and was exactly what Obasi and Henrik were looking for."

"I wouldn't get too optimistic," said Sean. "Let's just say you are not guaranteed to fail ... yet."

When we reached the room, Sean said, "One last thing. Whatever you do, don't sit at the table with them. Sit off on the side against the wall ... even if you have to sit on the floor. Better yet, don't sit at all, unless they invite you. Stand. They will think it more respectful. I'm told these people are very fussy about rank and privilege, and if you sit at the table, it is like telling them you think you're their equal. It's a tough audience." Sean checked his watch. "And today the meeting is bumped up tight against lunch. Worse, it's Friday: the day when, traditionally, senior leaders took some or all of their staff out for lunch as a group. Nothing like a room of bored and hungry executives to give your proposal lots of slack."

"It's nice to know that I can always count on you for such an upbeat view of people, because you always assume positive intent."

Sean shook his head. "I'm a realist. But you've got a great idea, and if we ignore this drama, it is the right thing to do."

There was an Admin sitting at the desk outside the conference room. I hadn't seen her before and she was dressed like she belonged in the more rarified spaces of the executive offices.

"Hi, my name is Chris. I'm here to present my initiative proposal to the PSIRB. Can I go right in"?

She looked up at me and said nothing. For a moment she just stared, then pointed to one of the nearby chairs and said, "Please have a seat. I will call you when they are ready for you."

Unlike Sabrina's PMO meeting, you weren't allowed into the PSIRB until it was your turn. I guess they didn't want you to pick up any cues from the prior presenters, or maybe they thought all of it was super secret because that was the world they lived in.

I was the last one presenting today, so there was no one to commiserate with outside the meeting, and the admin guarding the door made it quite clear she didn't want to chat with anyone ... at least not anyone below the executive level.

After about 20 minutes, the door opened, just enough for a woman to walk out. She was carrying a thick stack of documents and looking straight ahead.

"Hi, my name is Chris. How'd it go in there"?

She didn't acknowledge me, other than slowly shaking her head from side to side.

"Did you get approval"? I asked.

She turned and glared at me, but kept walking.

Shortly after she turned the corner, the admin guarding the door carefully laid down her pen and looking directly at me, said, "You may go in now."

This conference room was a long way from the Board Room IT would've used for something like this. This room was clean and tidy. In fact, it even smelled clean, as if there were a team dedicated to preventing the executives from being distracted from the business by any malodorous aromas.

The furniture was fresh and unworn. It even still had some of that fresh from the box new smell. The carpet was thick and plush, without the stains and tears I had come to expect in company conference rooms. Even the lighting felt exotic and expensive, with its carefully arranged spots and floods, all controlled in a myriad of combinations, by a panel of switches that looked like something out of a jumbo jet. And unlike the IT conference rooms, there were no crowds of people clustered around. There were only six people inside.

Three suits from the business I'd never seen before were sitting at the table. And I could not believe it. Adjacent to the three suits, at the table, sat Lee with the disgusting Cheshire Cat smile of his. He must have been here for all of the other presentations. How did he merit such treatment when I was left sitting outside?

There was really no place for me to sit, so I stood at the front of the room. It didn't matter; my presentation was only scheduled to last 20 minutes. I just hoped they wouldn't toss me out before I'd gone through it all.

None of the suits introduced themselves. I guess that in their hubris, they assumed that anyone who was important enough to merit their attention below them in the organization, would know who they were.

The one closest to me, in a very bored voice, said, "Proceed."

I quickly hooked my laptop to the projector, and, after one of the suits lowered the lights to accommodate the proposal projected on the screen at the far end of the room, I began. "My name is Chris. Thank you for giving me these minutes of your valuable time. The initiative I am proposing is driven by requests from the field organization. It will simplify the way they request IT services, improve the implementation time and alignment of those services, and allow the field to focus on their core goals, rather than needing to understand how IT works. By extending the legacy service catalog, so that it contains role-relevant views, the field will only need to work with services relevant to its goals and see them in language familiar to them."

None of the suits were paying any attention to me. One was staring at his watch, another was checking e-mail on her Smartphone, and the third was sitting there with her eyes closed. Even Lee was sending texts. And it was his group making the proposal. What kind of support was he giving me as my leader? I tried not to let the anger get the best of me, but he could hardly be less supportive. Maybe Sean was right: maybe he really did want me to fail, so he could use that as an excuse to fire me. But he'd never needed excuses for anyone else ... at least not that I knew of.

An instant later, I received a text, and, out of habit and without thinking, I pulled my phone out and checked it. The message was from Lee. I didn't understand until I read the brief content.

"This morning I accepted Crayton's resignation. He has gone off to start a new career and build his successes elsewhere."

The shock must have been noticeable on my face, because when I looked up at Lee, he winked. He had fired Crayton this morning, and was telling me now, in the middle of my presentation. Warning, threat, or just a shock bomb, it didn't matter. Lee was out to get me.

After that, the questions began almost immediately, and the ones from Lee were the worst. And when it became clear he had some issues, the suits jumped on me with both feet. It was the longest 15 minutes of my life, but I kept moving forward. I had worked too hard on this to let it go now, and I knew this was the right thing for the company.

I got to the end, and felt good about the proposal. No, I felt great about it. It was the best piece of work I had ever done, and I had focused the entire initiative down into a single page of how the enormous benefits to the field would clearly outweigh the minor increase in costs.

"Are there any questions"? I asked, and turned off the projector. Unfortunately, I had no idea of how to bring the rest of the lights up and stood there in the near darkness with everyone else.

After a split second of nothing but breathing, Lee spoke up.

"Abigail, Gunter, Murali .... please let me apologize to you."

The lights came up, and Lee was ignoring me and speaking directly to the suits.

"Chris works for me and I take full accountability for the evident lack of preparation invested in this presentation. Honestly, it looks like something he waited until late last night to begin work on. Frankly, I'm embarrassed and disappointed. We wish to withdraw this proposal, as it is not ready yet. Once it is up to our company's high standards, I will see to it that it is resubmitted for a proper evaluation. Again, I apologize for wasting your time today and accept full responsibility for Chris' failure here."

Abigail spoke up. "If you wish to withdraw the request for now, that is up to you, Lee. All of us have the highest regard for your judgment and focus on meeting the needs of the field. Something like this might make sense to begin as a development project in IT, and I think I speak for all of us when I say there is merit in this proposal, and, if ready, it probably should move forward immediately. However, we trust your assessment that now is not the time. The last thing we need is another disrupter in the field. We respect your taking accountability for the actions of your staff. It just reinforces to us the quality and effectiveness of your leadership."

Heads were nodding around the table. Lee was trying not to grin too much, and I was realizing that he was going to fire me today, right after this meeting. He had set me up, called me out as a failure in front of key executives, even though without him they probably would have approved it, and was going to improve his stature by taking accountability, handling the so-called tough assignment and then firing me.

As I walked out of the room and headed back toward my cube, it occurred to me that if it hadn't been so directly impacting, I could almost admire the Machiavellian beauty of Lee's actions. But now it was time to go and pack my office. I knew what was coming next.

Tips that would have helped Chris

Sometimes people succeed because they are good at what they do. But sometimes they succeed because they are lucky. Don't always assume that, because someone claims a win, it was due to their knowledge, skill, or capability. It could just as easily be due to luck, or being in the right place at the right time.

Sometimes your leadership will decide not to proceed with ITSM projects, even if they are the right thing to do, and will meet leadership's objectives. Being right, being the best, or being aligned with best practice, is not a guarantee others will see the light and want to adopt it. What becomes important then, is for you to continue to be an advocate for the change, to see how you can implement any parts of the change, even without approval, and most importantly, to not take it personally.

Some leaders advance their own careers by managing up. They spend much more of their time working with their leaders, than they do with the people reporting to them. This is often the sign of a weak or insecure leader. Plan ahead, and identify how you would work successfully for someone if you had only brief chunks of their time, and only on a schedule they set.

CHAPTER 15: NO GOOD DEED GOES UNPUNISHED

I had just started putting some of my personal effects into a box, when I got the call from Lee's admin, to meet him in his office immediately.

All the way there I kept vacillating between thinking I should beg to keep my job, and thinking it would do me more good just to tell him off, because he was going to fire me no matter what.

The door to Lee's office was open when I got there. He was on the phone as usual, but waved me in as he hung up.

"Please close the door behind you," he said.

Without waiting for an invitation, I threw myself down in a chair across the desk from him and said, "You really enjoy this, don't you"?

At this point I figured there was nothing left to lose. Legally, the company was governed by "Right to Work" laws which essentially gave them the right to terminate anyone at anytime, unless they were covered under a contract, like executives or union members. That left workers like myself quite disposable. If Lee wanted to fire me, there was absolutely nothing I could do about it.

"What happened to Crayton"? I asked.

Lee shook his head and said, "Personnel matters are private to protect the individual. Please show some empathy and respect for Crayton's privacy."

"So you fired him, just like you fired Ramesh, and for what? Not because they were doing the wrong things, but because you wanted to send a message. And now you plan to fire me."

"I am your manager, Chris, and it is my job to help you to be productive, and return an appropriate amount of value for the investment the company has made in you. Whether you approve of my style, or me personally, is not germane to our roles and obligations to the company. This is not personal. It is strictly business."

Lee opened a thick folder on his desk.

"Chris, we need to have a very serious discussion, one that may impact on your career at the company. So pay very close attention. I have here your personnel folder. As I am sure you are aware, it contains numerous reports of performance deficiencies in the months since you arrived, and a very unsatisfactory annual performance review that shows you failing to meet expectations ... "

"Horse Pucky!" I shouted. "I haven't had my review yet. It's not due for another 45 days."

"True, but human resources require managers to prepare performance reviews 45 days in advance, so they can be properly approved by senior leadership and HR. And while their contents are not normally reviewed until approved, I will tell you in the context of our discussion that the overall rating for you is failing to meet expectations."

Lee pulled out a handful of paper. "These represent specific individual situations where your performance has been substandard. And later today I will be writing one up for your pitiful performance this morning."

I leaned across the desk and jabbed my finger into the top of the desk. "You set me up. And when I was actually pulling it off, working my way out of your trap, you stepped in and stomped all over me in front of the executives."

"Actually, that merely shows your lack of awareness and experience working with senior leadership. By stopping their further consideration of your poorly constructed proposal, I saved you from the embarrassment of an immediate denial. You should be grateful I was there to help you."

I was tired of this. It was driving me crazy. I just wanted it over and to have Lee out of my life. "If you want to fire me, then just fire me. Don't try to justify it with a lot of nonsense."

"You may not believe this," he said, "but firing you is not the objective. Like all good managers at this company, I want you to be a productive contributor to our mutual success. It's just that in your case, you seem to lack either the focus or the capability."

Lee pulled a thin folder from his desk. It held two sheets of paper. Laying them down side by side facing me, so that I could read them, he pushed one towards me. It was a letter already written under my name.

"Because I think you have potential, I am giving you two choices. First, is the option to resign today, effective immediately. If you choose that option, I have arranged for you to receive two weeks' severance pay and continue your medical coverage until the end of the month. There will be no negative references given."

Lee patted the larger, thick folder. "And this file will remain sealed. So it will not impact your ability to succeed elsewhere."

He pulled that document back across the table to him and pushed the other one toward me.

"As an alternative, I have here a remedial performance plan for you that spells out specific goals and behaviors you must achieve in the next 30 days. If you are successful, those accomplishments will be recorded in your personnel file, and you will remain an employee of the company until such time as you decide to leave, or you fail to maintain these high standards."

I looked at the list of items. All were highly subjective, at the mercy of Lee's moods. And those that were not, were arbitrary, and had little to do with my work. It was a list set up in such a way that I would never be able to achieve it; especially not in 30 days.

"And what happens if I can't meet these in 30 days"?

Lee pulled the document back and pointed to a section at the bottom. "If you fail to meet the commitment at any time during the 30 day period, you will be terminated with no severance, no further medical coverage, and these documents will remain accessible in your file for any future employers who call seeking references."

Lee put the paper back in the folder and added, "And so there is no misunderstanding, the decision to terminate does not need to wait the full 30 days. It can be put into action anytime after it is signed, at the discretion of your manager, who is me."

I shook my head. "So you could fire me the next day if you wished."

"That's looking at it the wrong way. The performance plan is there to help you apply your full capabilities, to our common goals. It's not a vast conspiracy out to get you. You've been watching too much television."

"Was this the same offer you made to Ramesh and Crayton? Did they chose the faux chance at rehabilitation, or did they choose to slip out quietly"?

Lee shook his head. "You're asking about matters that don't concern you, and just by asking them, you're reinforcing how difficult it will be for you to achieve the listed improvements in 30 days."

Lee stood up, came around to my side of the desk, and sat in the chair beside me. "As a manager, I've dealt with a lot of these types of situations before. Let me offer you some advice. You are a good person, and I don't want to see you stress out. Just by listening to you, I can tell there is no way you are going to be able to make it through the 30 days successfully. I seriously doubt if you will make it past Monday. Save yourself some pain. Save your dignity. Sign the resignation letter and set yourself free. There are places out there better suited to you."

That was perfect for Lee. I resign and there is none of the mess of a firing, and he gets credit for being a firm but fair manager who's looking out for the good of the field. Maybe I should quit and start a consulting company with Ramesh and Crayton. We could call ourselves "The Burnt Ends."

"Unfortunately," said Lee, and he placed both documents before me. "I need a decision from you today, before you leave this room. What is your choice"?

I hesitated. Every bit of me said resign, take the money and run away from the pain. But after all the suffering Lee had put me through, I needed to fight back, to somehow even up the score.

"I want the 30-day remedial performance plan. I am confident I can achieve it."

"You understand this is a very aggressive plan, and you will be eligible for termination at any time after you sign it"?

I nodded, more confident now. "Yes, although I'd like to go over it with human resources. And why aren't they here"?

"They will be here soon. You need to get a signature down before they arrive," said Lee, as he retrieved the resignation letter and extended a pen. He pointed with a finger to the line on the performance plan. "If this is your choice, sign here, please."

I stared at the signatory line for a second, before inking my name, and the date. I pushed it back across the desk to Lee, and he did the same.

As if on cue, the door opened, and Helmut, the head of HR, stuck his head in. "May I intrude"?

"No intrusion," said Lee. "Your timing is excellent. We've just made our decision."

"Excellent," he said. "But before we finalize that," he opened the door completely. Standing beside him was Jessica, our CIO, and Joshua, our CEO. "We need to have a very serious discussion. Your office may be a little small. There is a conference room down the hall."

"Of course," said Lee, and he stood up and headed for the door. He handed my signed remedial performance plan agreement to Helmut.

I stood up, and began to follow Lee, but Helmut stopped me. He checked his watch and said, "Right now we need to verify a few things with Lee. It's late. We'll update you and your status on Monday morning. You may return to your work."

I sat in Lee's office for a few moments after they had all left, and wondered if I had made the right choice. Maybe all I'd done is move my firing day from Friday to Monday. I wasn't sure. But I did know that I had made life a little more complicated for Lee, and although I'd never been into payback before, this felt really good.

I left Lee's office, but never went back to my cube. I headed for the parking lot and headed out to get a glass of beer. I figured I was owed one.

Monday morning came too quickly for me. As I walked up to the door I hesitated before swiping my ID card. I wondered if it was going to work, or if, after their meeting on Friday, Lee had already gotten me fired. With a deep breath, I swiped my card, and to my surprise, the door opened as it always had. So far, so good.

I hadn't received any e-mails or text messages from Lee, so I headed over to his office to see what the next steps would be.

When I got there, no one was around. I knocked on the door and got no response, so I pushed it open. The entire room was empty. No boxes, no furniture, no awards, no expensive furniture ... nothing. It was so empty, it almost echoed.

I was standing there, totally confused, when I heard footsteps behind me. I turned around. It was Sean.

"I guess no one told you, did they"? asked Sean.

"Told me what"? I asked.

"You probably don't read your e-mail in the morning, either. In case you've lost your sight, Lee is gone."

I was stupefied. "You mean set free to succeed in other ventures"?

"No, he wasn't fired. Actually, he was moved back to the field."

I started to smile. So they sent him home because he didn't play well with others. That was almost worth being on probation. Maybe even that would be lifted, too. "So there is some justice, after all."

Sean laughed. "I'm sure he'd see it that way. He's been promoted. He's now in charge of all operations for an entire division in the field. Everything: sales, service, support, the works, all report ultimately to him in the region. He's one step away from making VP. Apparently they had been considering this for a while and after his "success" working with IT here in home office, the powers that be decided he could lead the entire operation."

"You're kidding," I mumbled.

"Check your e-mail. I think he is even the youngest person in the company's history to get that much responsibility."

Sean gave me a slap on the back. "You may have had the privilege of working directly for our next CEO in training. How does that feel"?

I wanted to break something. But before I could do anything, Jessica, our CIO, walked by. "There you are, Chris. We've been looking all over for you. I need to see you in my office right away. With Lee's promotion out, you will be temporarily reporting directly to me. We have some very serious discussions to have about achieving the goals related to your remedial performance plan. Can you come with me now back to my office"?

I nodded yes and started to follow her. Sean whispered, "Good luck."

We walked quickly. Jessica was a leader with a lot to do and she moved fast to get it done.

We were about half way there when she asked me, "I also need to talk to you about any prior experience you've had managing direct reports, or working with dashboards, key performance indicators, metrics and scorecards."

Tips that would have helped Chris

As you begin a series of ITSM initiatives, there will be some where you will not win, you will not get approval to proceed, and you will not get credit for all the work; no matter how good your initiative is. It will not matter how right or aligned your proposal may be. Never give up. Be persistent.

ITG RESOURCES

IT Governance Ltd sources, creates and delivers products and services to meet the real-world, evolving IT governance needs of today's organisations, directors, managers and practitioners.

The ITG website (*www.itgovernance.co.uk*) is the international one-stop-shop for corporate and IT governance information, advice, guidance, books, tools, training and consultancy. On the website you will find the following pages related to IT service management and the subject matter of this book:

www.itgovernance.co.uk/itsm.aspx

www.itgovernance.co.uk/iso20000.aspx

www.itgovernance.co.uk/itil.aspx.

Publishing Services

IT Governance Publishing (ITGP) is the world's leading IT-GRC publishing imprint that is wholly owned by IT Governance Ltd.

With books and tools covering all IT governance, risk and compliance frameworks, we are the publisher of choice for authors and distributors alike, producing unique and practical publications of the highest quality, in the latest formats available, which readers will find invaluable.

www.itgovernancepublishing.co.uk is the website dedicated to ITGP. Other titles published by ITGP that may be of interest include:

- The Daniel McLean ITSM Fiction Series

  www.itgovernance.co.uk/shop/p-1526.aspx

- The ITSM Thought Leadership Series

  www.itgovernance.co.uk/shop/p-1398.aspx

- ITIL Lifecycle Essentials

www.itgovernance.co.uk/shop/p-1285.aspx.

We also offer a range of off-the-shelf toolkits that give comprehensive, customisable documents to help users create the specific documentation they need to properly implement a management system or standard. Written by experienced practitioners and based on the latest best practice, ITGP toolkits can save months of work for organisations working towards compliance with a given standard.

Toolkits that may be of interest include:

- ITSM, ITIL® & ISO/IEC 20000 Implementation Toolkit

  www.itgovernance.co.uk/shop/p-872.aspx

- IT Governance Control Framework Implementation Toolkit

  www.itgovernance.co.uk/shop/p-1305.aspx

- ISO/IEC 20000 Documentation Toolkit

  www.itgovernance.co.uk/shop/p-632.aspx.

Books and tools published by IT Governance Publishing (ITGP) are available from all business booksellers and the following websites:

www.itgovernance.eu   *www.itgovernanceusa.com*

www.itgovernance.in   *www.itgovernancesa.co.za*

www.itgovernance.asia.

Training Services

IT Governance offers an extensive portfolio of training courses designed to educate information security, IT governance, risk management and compliance professionals.

ISO/IEC 20000 is the first International Standard for IT service management and has been developed to reflect the best practice guidance contained within the ITIL framework. Our ISO20000 Foundation and Practitioner training courses are designed to provide delegates with a comprehensive introduction and guide to the implementation of an ISO20000 management system and an industry recognised qualification awarded by APMG International.

We also have a unique ITIL Foundation (2 Day) training course designed to provide delegates with the knowledge and skills required to pass the EXIN ITIL Foundation examination at the very first attempt.

Full details of all IT Governance training courses can be found at *www.itgovernance.co.uk/training.aspx*.

Professional Services and Consultancy

Our expert consultants can show you how to best apply the lessons of ITIL, COBIT and ISO/IEC 20000 so that you can make process improvements and eliminate any 'gaps'. We explain the ideal and purpose behind each framework and then help you to find the most appropriate solutions to create a stronger and more robust Service Management System (SMS). By drawing on our extensive experience of management systems to combine service management frameworks, you can support the goal of delivering quality services that benefit the business - efficiently, effectively and economically.

We can coach you in the most effective ways to conduct enterprise-wide assessments. With our support, you will learn to describe the often complex interrelationships between different processes, recognizing and taking account of the various maturity levels.

For more information about IT Governance Consultancy for IT service management, see *www.itgovernance.co.uk/itsm-itil-iso20000-consultancy.aspx*.

ITG Resources

Newsletter

IT governance is one of the hottest topics in business today, not least because it is also the fastest moving.

You can stay up to date with the latest developments across the whole spectrum of IT governance subject matter, including; risk management, information security, ITIL and IT service management, project governance, compliance and so much more, by subscribing to ITG's core publications and topic alert emails.

Simply visit our subscription centre and select your preferences: *www.itgovernance.co.uk/newsletter.aspx.*

EU for product safety is Stephen Evans, The Mill Enterprise Hub, Stagreenan, Drogheda, Co. Louth, A92 CD3D, Ireland. (servicecentre@itgovernance.eu)

www.ingramcontent.com/pod-product-compliance
Lightning Source LLC
Chambersburg PA
CBHW071119050326
40690CB00008B/1269